The Command Decisions Series

• VOLUME 5 •
Aircraft Performance

The Command Decisions Series • Volume 5

Aircraft Performance

The Forces Without

Richard L. Taylor

Belvoir Publications, Inc.
Greenwich, Connecticut

Also by Richard L. Taylor

IFR for VFR Pilots: An Exercise in Survival
Understanding Flying
Instrument Flying
Fair-Weather Flying
Recreational Flying
Positive Flying (with William Guinther)
The First Flight
Pilot's Audio Update (Editor)

ISBN: 1-879620-07-3

Printed and bound in the United States of America by Arcata Graphics (Fairfield, Pennsylvania).

Contents

Preface

"Kick tire, light fire, show me the go-handle"...the jet fighter pilot's preflight checklist. Tongue in cheek, of course, but it harkens back to older days when military airplanes were much less complex, the pilots a bit more cavalier, and the consequences of a tire-kicking preflight weren't so sinister.

The importance of thorough preflight inspections is taught from Day One of flight training, and most pilots continue to be good checkers throughout their aviation careers. Nonetheless, there is so much to look for—sometimes things that can make the difference between a pleasant flight experience and a catastrophe—that we have selected a number of articles and case histories from *Aviation Safety* to help you do a better job of preflight inspections. That pretty much describes the first part of this volume.

In the second part, we'll take a look at performance, a somewhat more complex topic. When a pilot opens the throttle for takeoff, he expects things to happen. It may be nothing more than the soft push of 100 horses getting a two-seat trainer underway, but regardless of the powerplant involved, x amount of thrust should propel y amount of weight down the runway and cause it to become airborne in z number of feet.

At the other end of a flight, a pilot expects that crossing the runway threshold at a specific height and in a specific configuration will bring the airplane to a stop in the distance found in the handbook; x amount of braking power should stop y number of pounds in z number of feet.

These are simple physical laws at work. And between these two very obvious demonstrations are as many facets of performance as there are things your airplane can do; climb, turn, burn fuel, descend, glide—you name it—there's a chart or table or procedure to help you arrive at a reasonable expectation of aircraft behavior.

The objective of the second part of this fifth volume in the

Command Decision series is to acquaint you—or re-acquaint, as the case may be—with the various aspects of aircraft performance that impact day-to-day flight operations. We will also spend some time discussing emergency situations, when optimum performance can sometimes save the day; at the least, knowledge of how to get the most out of your airplane and the ability to apply it will most likely improve the outcome of any abnormal episode.

You'll also find information dealing with performance charts and how to use them, critical preflight considerations (mostly loading procedures), engine performance, short-field and soft-field takeoff and landing techniques, and a comprehensive review of flight procedures for light twins...with both engines running and with one of the powerplants failed. *(A special note of caution and a disclaimer:* We have used a number of airplane performance charts and tables throughout this volume. They are typical, and taken from real airplane handbooks—but they are intended for illustration only, may not be current, and are not to be used in any way for determining or predicting actual performance.)

Lack of performance—in other words, when the airplane can't deliver what's required to accomplish a specific task—often results in a tragic accident, sometimes merely an embarrassing mishap. As we've done throughout the *Command Decision Series,* we'll season these discussions with case histories—actual situations in which performance played a role.

Richard Taylor
Dublin, Ohio
August 20, 1991

Preflight Operations and Inspections

It sounds like one of those "urban legends," but as far as we can tell it's a true story. A pilot took off in his Bonanza one day, and hadn't gotten very far into the air when he noticed that the airplane seemed unusually tail-heavy, and no wonder—he had neglected to free it from its tiedown and was dragging an automobile tire filled with concrete through the air.

Then there's the tale of the 2nd Lieutenant in Air Force flight training who added progressively more power to his T-6, but it still wouldn't move away from the parking space. The racket (there's no way to power-up a T-6 quietly) caught the attention of a veteran crew chief who climbed up on the wing, tapped the fledgling pilot on the shoulder and said, "Son, she'd go a lot better if you'd untie the tailwheel."

These incidents speak to the structural strength of the aircraft involved, but they don't say much for the pilots and their preflight inspections—or lack thereof. "The preflight" has been with us since the very beginning, and is no less important to safe flight operations today than it was when flyers had to check every piece of wood and every turnbuckle to make sure the airplane would stay together. True, contemporary aircraft are much better constructed and more reliable than their forebears, and good design permits an airplane to return its occupants safely to earth following inflight failures that would have crashed earlier machines, but the fact remains that a good preflight inspection usually uncovers a problem before it gets out of hand.

The pilot of the Cessna 421C had a reputation for depending on others to make sure the airplane was ready for flight. He had instructed line-service personnel at the small airport north of Albuquerque to keep the engine oil at the proper level, and to always top off the fuel tanks after a flight. He was observed on many occasions to arrive at the airport in a hurry, get on board and go—no preflight inspection at all.

The accident flight began just like that; four passengers and their snow-skiing equipment were loaded quickly, and away they went. Nobody noticed that after the skis were placed in the nose compartment, one of the doors was left unlatched.

A number of witnesses saw the 421 take off, and at rotation, the nose baggage door came open because of the change in airflow around the nose when the pitch attitude was changed. The runway was long enough to accept an abort at that point—not a lot of extra concrete, but enough—but the pilot elected to continue...and he did so in a manner that clearly indicated he was anxious to get back on the ground as rapidly as possible. Witnesses watched as the airplane entered a steep bank to the left and continued to climb onto a downwind leg. The wheels remained extended throughout the episode, obviously in anticipation of an immediate landing.

When the Cessna reached normal pattern altitude at mid-field, the pilot apparently decided to shut down the right engine to eliminate the possibility of propeller damage if a ski or two came out of the baggage compartment. Not a bad idea, but if everything had stayed in place up to this point, the chances were good that it would remain where it was the rest of the way.

Workers on a rooftop directly below the airplane recounted a reduction in sound, then total silence. Others who watched indicated a pronounced yaw and a rapid turn, then a steep descent on a path perpendicular to the runway. The 421 clipped a row of trees before it slammed into the southbound lanes of an interstate highway, bounced over the median and came to rest in a field on the other side. The impact may have been survivable, but a fire started

It's almost axiomatic that every flight starts with a careful preflight. Yet each year, a number of accidents are caused by mechanical deficiencies that should have been detected during preflight.

and consumed the cabin before the people could get out.

Despite the damage, conclusive evidence remained. The left prop blades were feathered (the corresponding lever was in the feather detent), and the right throttle was closed. Could it be true that the pilot had throttled back on the right engine (sound reduction) in anticipation of shutting down that engine, then feathered the left propeller (total silence)? Subsequent flight tests showed that the airplane would have behaved exactly as it did in that configuration—a disaster that could have been averted with a decent preflight inspection.

Some pilots are tire-kickers who are satisfied to see that wings, engines and wheels are in place, some are perfectionists who check every rivet every time. Somewhere between those extremes is a satisfactory preflight inspection, but most important is a pilot's resolve to always check at least the critical items. One of Murphy's many laws of aviation states, "If anything on an airplane can come

Most twins, Cessna's 421 included, will fly just fine with a door or baggage compartment open, as long as the pilot doesn't become preoccupied before he or she can land.

loose, it will...and always at the wrong time." Merely rapping on the cowling during the walkaround can uncover a potentially dangerous problem, as this accident shows:

> The worst possible time to suffer a partial power loss is shortly after takeoff, when there's insufficient runway remaining to land straight ahead and not enough power to climb. The combination of low altitude and low airspeed make for a situation that's difficult to escape unscathed. A student pilot in a Piper PA-28-180 Cherokee got an object lesson in this truism one afternoon and barely made it back to the airport. The pilot was unhurt, but the airplane suffered substantial damage.
>
> The Cherokee was based at El Monte, California, and the pilot, who was also half-owner, arrived at the airport to find his partner and flight instructor just returned from a flight. They were planning to be on the ground for some time before flying again, so they suggested he take the airplane up for some pattern work. The weather was very good, with light winds and high, scattered clouds.

The pilot performed a preflight, walking around the plane, checking fuel and oil, and taxied to Runway 19 for takeoff. Everything was normal until the Cherokee reached 100 feet AGL, when the left side of the engine cowling popped open and began to flutter. The pilot immediately called the tower and declared an emergency, saying that he was going to return to the airport, whereupon the controller cleared him to land on Runway 1.

The pilot discovered that a reduced throttle setting caused the flutter to cease, and the cowling stabilized at about a 45-degree angle, partially blocking his vision. The low power setting brought the airplane close to a stall, but with few choices, the pilot continued at the reduced power setting.

It was then he noticed power lines ahead of him. He was too close to go over the wires, so he tried to fly between them, the propeller cut one wire and the Cherokee's tail caught the other. The impact with the wire severely damaged the tail, and made the rudder inoperative.

The pilot somehow maintained control after the collision, and was barely able to maintain level flight with the reduced power setting. He executed a gentle right turn at an altitude of about 40 feet AGL and an airspeed of 55 to 60 mph. "The stall light was blinking on and off," the pilot later said. He was able to make a normal, full-flap landing on Runway 1.

Subsequent investigation revealed no defect in the Dzus-type cowling latch mechanism. The pilot said that he did not open the cowl during his preflight, nor did he specifically check the latches. Since the accident, he has altered the fasteners to make them more difficult to open.

Cowling plugs are used by lots of pilots whose airplanes are parked outside. They are intended to keep birds and other foreign objects out of the engine, and they do a great job; but they must be removed before flight. As a matter of fact, some cowling plugs carry those words—REMOVE BEFORE FLIGHT—and often sport bright red streamers that wave in the breeze and alert a pilot to their presence.

Even if a pilot did no more of a preflight inspection than stand

The Dzus-type fasteners on Cherokee cowlings become worn with age. Careful preflight will reveal one that's about to let go.

in front of his airplane and count the wings and wheels, you'd think he'd notice that the cowling plugs had not been removed. Not this pilot; he apparently was able to get the engine started, taxi, and take off with the plugs still in place. But it was a short flight.

The Cessna 210 crashed—no survivors—when the engine lost power shortly after takeoff and the pilot tried to get back to the airport. The private pilot had logged approximately 400 hours, half of that in the Cessna 210.

Investigators said the airplane departed on Runway 9 and shortly after lift-off the engine started losing power. The pilot tried to bring the Cessna around and land in the opposite direction, but the aircraft was too low. It glanced off a junked car in a junkyard off the end of the runway, ran through a fence, and crashed on the runway threshold. A

The cord connecting two cowl plugs should be looped over the prop so the plugs will be pulled out if the engine is accidentally started with the plugs still in place.

fire broke out and the Cessna was destroyed.

Investigators found a set of cowling plugs in the wreckage. One was attached to the propeller, and the cord which connected the two plugs was wrapped around the prop shaft. The other plug was found farther forward in the wreckage path. Investigators believe the pilot left the plugs in the cowling intakes during takeoff, leading to severe engine overheating and the loss of power on takeoff.

The NTSB investigator interviewed the co-owner of the Cessna, who said he had placed the plugs in the cowling after his last flight. He recalled that the cord that connects the two plugs was under and behind the propeller when he left it. According to the investigator, if the cord had been left above and in front of the propeller, the plugs would have been pulled out of the cowling when the engine started.

One pilot told us of the steps his school is taking to develop healthy habits in students and renters. "We make *sure* people do preflights," he told us. "Even if you own an XYZ aircraft and you want to rent our XYZ, we make sure you're checked out on the preflight. We build strong preflight habits in our students and renters."

Unfortunately, a weekend at almost any airport will show that many pilots and FBOs tend to pass over the preflight. Many flight instructors, after showing the preflight to the student once or twice, stay in the office and drink coffee, allowing the student to perform the inspection with no supervision. This also allows the formation of habits that will carry through the rest of a flying career.

One pilot who encountered the hazards of habits has vowed to change his procedures for refueling. He learned a lesson on the value of more than "cursory preflights" after an encounter with water in the fuel system of a Bellanca 8KCAB Decathlon.

This pilot and a friend had planned to spend an hour doing some aerobatics in the local area. They arrived at the airport to find the Bellanca waiting at the fuel pumps, and put 7.5 gallons into each wing. The pilot would later recount, "I did my usual cursory walkaround, draining fuel from the engine sump, the wings, and the undercarriage— the low point, where any moisture would collect. The procedure was, as usual, to let the supposed water droplets and fuel fall to the ground."

The rest of the preflight looked good, so they taxied out and took off, and about 75 feet in the air, the engine sputtered and died. They maneuvered toward a road and crash-landed in a snowbank, injuring both pilots and badly damaging the Bellanca.

The pilot later learned that of the 15 gallons of liquid pumped into the tanks, six gallons were water. In his own words, "The water would have been difficult if not impossible to detect. It would have been suspended in the fuel after the agitation of going through the pump."

The pilot subsequently vowed that would never happen to him again. "I'll find something to strain fuel into, no matter what...but I won't fly again within ten minutes of taking on fuel. I'll give the water a chance to settle, along with my peace of mind."

Test the fuel after every refueling, no matter how confident you are of the fuel source and pump filters.

Pilots have the ultimate responsibility for every detail of a preflight but they are not necessarily getting the best of help from the airplane manufacturers. Virtually all flight manuals (even prior to the GAMA format days), have contained a "preflight checklist," putatively intended to help the pilot do a thorough job on his preflight. In fact, we have yet to discover a checklist in any manual sufficiently detailed that a pilot could discover most conceivable flaws in an airplane, and certainly no manual adequately warns of the hazards of various common mechanical discrepancies. To quote from a typical flight manual, regarding what a pilot should do when he arrives at the left wing trailing edge:

Flap—check
Aileron—check
Wingtip—check
Position light—check

Mufflers and exhaust pipes frequently vibrate and loosen. A vigorous shake of the pipes will reveal problems.

Of course, this advice is left totally open to interpretation. The pilot may check to see that he has all of the specified appliances—"Yes, I do have a wingtip." The pilot could also check the condition of the items as far as he is able to guess the potential flaws that might be there. But as for the actual things that might go wrong with ailerons and wingtips, the manual contains no advice at all.

Sometimes, major hazards are caught by the chance fingering of some normally overlooked part. Airplanes are such complex machines—fragile in some areas and rugged in others—that some pilots may be reluctant to touch their airplanes. Sometimes they literally don't know what they're missing.

A pilot was preflighting a Piper Arrow, and when it came time to check the nosewheel assembly, he crouched under the cowling and examined the wheel well. Gripping the exhaust to steady himself, he noticed it felt loose. He gave it a little shake, but decided it was okay.

He continued his preflight, and finding the rest of the aircraft in good order, climbed aboard to fire up. As the engine turned over and caught, he thought he heard a funny noise. The thought of the exhaust stack returned, and he shut down to find the right exhaust had come off. As it turned out, the nuts holding the stack in place had backed out, allowing it to disconnect.

This pilot now shakes the exhaust pipe as part of every preflight.

The pilot of a Beech Baron evidently did not check the security of the exhaust system during his preflight inspection at a California airport, and the result was a fatal accident just after takeoff. The Baron had lifted off and made an immediate left turn as the pilot radioed he was returning to the airport. The left bank steepened until the aircraft rolled inverted, dove into the roof of an airport building and exploded, killing all aboard. After the accident, the exhaust stack from the left engine was found lying on the taxiway where the Baron had started its takeoff run. Investigation showed the clamps holding the exhaust pipe in place had worked loose.

Beware That First Flight

Life-threatening problems can show up on an aircraft fresh out of the shop for major maintenance or a paint job. During the course of maintenance, many things such as access panels, ailerons, engine accessories and such, are removed to permit work. Sometimes, they're not put back as they should be. During our talks with pilots around the country, we came across several instances of this.

One prime example involved the owner of a Beech B55 Baron. He had taken the plane to a field near Boston for repainting, and upon completion of the work, flew it about 100 miles to his home field.

A local mechanic happened to look the airplane over, and noticed something the owner hadn't; the aileron skin was not screwed into the top hinge plate. During reinstallation of the aileron, paint shop personnel had "missed" with the aileron attach screws, driving them not into the hinge plate holes, but alongside the plate. Because the upper edge of the hinge plate was pushing against the screw as it went in, it had the same feel as though it were in the hole. In essence, the upper skin of the aileron was not attached.

Aviation Safety spoke with the mechanic who found the mis-hung aileron, and he offered some very good advice for preflight inspections. "It's not enough to waggle the ailerons on a preflight," he said, "rather, it's also smart to pull gently fore and aft, so as to check whether it's attached to the hinges. Most pilots will lift an aileron or elevator and look at the hinge pins for security, but very few will look to see if the surface is actually attached to the hinge. If they just give it a pull, they'll see."

The Baron pilot can count himself lucky to have flown home and not encountered any control or flutter problems. Luck held for the pilot of another twin, this one based in California, and also just out of the paint shop. When he arrived after flying the airplane home, the pilot's friends and acquaintances came out to admire the new finish. As the well-wishers gawked, one of them remarked, "Gee, that aileron is hanging funny."

"You know," the pilot replied, "it flew strange, too. It seemed to need a lot of aileron trim to stay level." A quick check revealed that his aileron had also been hung incorrectly.

Another mechanic, after having found problems with the elevator torque tube adapters on several aircraft, offered some preflight advice for pilots of Cessna singles. During an inspection, this mechanic had found loose or sheared rivets used to secure the adapters to the elevator torque tube. According to his report, "this condition can be detected by holding one elevator immobile while attempting to move the other. Any movement indicates that looseness is present." He specifically pointed out Cessna 172, 180, 182, 185, 188, and 200 series aircraft as candidates for this procedure.

Post-paint job surprises don't always end up with such mild results. The pilot of an A-100 King Air picked up the aircraft from the paint shop, and after liftoff for the flight home tried to raise the landing gear. The wheels came up part of the way and stopped, the retraction motor burned out, and further attempts with the normal gear system were fruitless. The pilot then tried the manual extension system, but this was also jammed. He was finally able to pry the nose-wheel chain off the gear in the manual extension gearbox and lower the main wheels, but the nose gear remained retracted, resulting in substantial damage during the landing.

Investigation of the landing gear system found the nose gear actuator had been jammed by a piece of masking tape that had been put on the actuator shaft during the repainting. A minor detail had led to major damages, and could have been detected by an extra-thorough preflight.

Similarly, Piper Seneca pilots have found that if the shimmy damper bolt on the nose wheel is installed upside down (this has been done on several occasions), it hangs up on the nose-wheel door actuator tube, effectively locking the gear in the up position. Although the damages incurred from the ensuing nosegear-up landing are not usually life-threatening, the import of this episode has probably not been lost on the unlucky owners who have experienced it. As an aid to the pilot, if not the mechanic, there is now (or should be) a placard near the nosegear describing the proper installation of the bolt.

Gear Downers

When it comes to retractable landing gear, extra scrutiny of all the parts can ease the strain on the pilot, and save much wear and tear on the aircraft. The pilot of a Piper Apache found himself faced with a gear-up landing after the nut holding the nosewheel came off after departure, cocking the wheel in the well and holding the gear up. In his anxiety to limit damage to the engines on touchdown, he feathered the props too soon and undershot the landing. Had he put as much effort into the preflight, perhaps he would have noticed the loose nut and the accident could have been prevented with the twist of a wrench.

An East Coast flight instructor told of finding a loose nut on the nosewheel of her flight school's trainer by going the extra inch during a preflight. "I looked at it and it didn't look right. So I grabbed it and found it was less than finger tight. We could have lost the nosewheel if we hadn't caught that," she said.

Steering mechanisms may also deserve an extra look or two. A pilot on the West Coast told us of an encounter with a broken steering mechanism on a Cessna 172. During his preflight, he bent down to check the inflation of the nosegear oleo strut, and noticed something hanging down. It looked out of place, and it was; it turned out to be the steering control link. It had broken from its bracket and was hanging out of the opening where it exited the cowling.

Unseen Events

Sometimes, while the pilot's away, the gremlins play. Faults and failures seem to appear from out of nowhere. More often, however, they have a definite (human) cause, and only extra care during the preflight can prevent unpleasant surprises.

For example, overzealous line personnel can precipitate a problem for pilots of Mooney M20 series aircraft—nosegear collapse. The Mooney's nosegear linkages permit the nosewheel to be turned through a rather small radius during ground handling. Line personnel attempting to maneuver a Mooney in tight quarters might swing the tow bar too far, resulting in dents in the nosegear brace, which can weaken the structure enough to let the nosegear collapse on the next landing. For those willing to make the effort to crouch down and examine the nosegear assembly closely, the dents are readily apparent.

Sometimes the gremlins lurk under the pilot's hat...

The pilot of a Mitsubishi MU-2B preflighted his airplane in a hangar because of heavy rains, and found nothing unusual. When it came time to move the aircraft out of the hangar, the pilot got help from some maintenance people and together they moved out an airplane which was blocking the MU-2. They then disconnected the nosegear scissors on the MU-2 to make the towing easier. (Disconnecting the scissors allows the nosewheel to swivel freely, a common practice with these airplanes.)

When the MU-2 was finally out of the hangar, the maintenance people asked the pilot to help move the other aircraft back inside. They hurried in the pouring rain and pushed it back in. Afterwards, the pilot boarded his passenger and taxied out for takeoff.

Using differential thrust and braking, he was able to taxi out and take off. But as soon as the gear handle was moved to "retract," he knew instantly that he had forgotten to reconnect the nosegear. The gear would not come up.

He flew to another airport to burn off fuel for the landing, which was complicated by a slight crosswind from the right. When the MU-2 touched down, it began to veer off to the left, then veered some more to the left, then ran off the runway and sustained substantial damage.

In his accident report, the 29,000-hour ATP commented, "Pilots should be especially aware when distracted from standard operating procedure. In this case (not an excuse, but an explanation), distraction at the point of normal connection of the nosewheel scissors contributed to the cause of the accident."

Troublesome Trim Tabs

Small and easy to overlook, the trim tabs on various control surfaces can spell trouble if they're not working as advertised, or not connected properly. At the least, tab problems can make for an uncomfortable flight with the pilot holding constant pressure against a poorly trimmed surface. At worst, they can produce flutter and airframe failure. With only a little extra attention during the preflight, most trim tab troubles can be readily detected.

A flight instructor flying Cessna 150s shared an experience with us which he says taught him a valuable lesson about trim systems. He and a student had completed the preflight and runup and called the tower, ready to take off. They had set the elevator trim by moving the cockpit indicator to the correct position.

As the Cessna gathered speed on the takeoff, it suddenly broke ground and climbed at a very steep angle. The CFI chided his student for over-rotating, but the student replied that he was forcing the yoke forward against considerable nose-up pressure.

Although the trim indicator was in the takeoff position, the instructor rolled in what appeared to be full nose-down trim, whereupon the 150 became its usual, docile self, and they brought it around and landed.

After shutting down, they found that the trim tab was now in about the correct position, but the indicator tab was buried in the front of the indicator (beyond full nose-down trim).

"The only thing I could figure," the instructor said, "was that someone had operated the trim with something sticking in the indicator. This probably bent the little indicator tab so that it didn't align with the actual position of the trim tab. Now, as a part of every preflight, I set the trim to the takeoff position and go back and look at the tab to check its position. On a 150, it's not serious if it's out of line, but on something bigger, it could be fatal."

On most two-door trainers, rolling in full nose-up trim at the start of the preflight inspection makes it easy to confirm that the tab moves in the correct direction (down, in the case of a typical elevator-equipped airplane) and the correct amount. Upon reaching the other side of the airplane, full nose-down trim can be rolled in (which moves the tab up) and again the tab's operation can be checked.

One pilot who should have made such a check of his trim system did not get the chance to make a habit of it. He and his four passengers were killed when his Beech Baron crashed into a tractor trailer and a warehouse while attempting to return to the airport.

The stage for the accident was set several days earlier when a mechanic had worked on the trim system and swapped the elevator trim actuators. This had the effect of creating nose-down trim when the pilot called for nose-up. Making matters worse, the swapped trim actuators permitted much greater-than-normal nose-down travel of the trim tabs, and the forces generated by them. The Baron was out of control when it plowed into the truck and building. Investigators found the trim tabs in the full nose-down position.

> The pilot of a Piper Aztec found himself confronted with some "gremlin-induced" trim-tab damage that almost killed him. His aircraft was tied down at a metropolitan New York airport and late one evening, a line person in a hurry backed a fuel truck into the Aztec's stabilizer. The trim tab was bent downward almost 90 degrees. The driver, either frightened of the consequences or completely ignorant of what he had done, simply pulled away from the airplane and completed his fueling rounds.
>
> The following evening was a classic "dark and stormy night." The Aztec pilot showed up for a flight, and hurried through his preflight in the darkness and rain. He failed to

notice the bent trim tab—until he tried to take off.

As the airplane gathered speed, the tab became quite effective. The nose reached a dangerously high attitude and the Aztec was rapidly heading for a stall just off the deck. With full power and full nose-up elevator, it entered the clouds.

The pilot reacted quickly and used his knees to hold the yoke forward while bringing the Aztec around for a successful landing. There is no doubt the damage was the truck driver's fault, and there is also no doubt that the pilot's preflight inspection left something to be desired.

Maintaining Controls

Thorough inspection of the flight controls can preclude possibly disastrous encounters, as a Piper Seneca pilot discovered. During his preflight, he checked the ailerons closely and noticed a longitudinal crack in the left aileron hinge bearing. He notified his mechanic, who inspected the controls more closely, and found cracks in all six hinge bearings. There were several possible consequences had the pilot taken off—frozen, bound or excessively stiff controls, or possibly even having the control surfaces come off in flight.

There's also the specter of misconnections. As remote as the possibility of reversed controls seems to most pilots, two experienced Piper production test pilots were caught in this fatal trap on the initial flight of a brand-new Navajo.

They were not hurried—they were observed to spend some 15 minutes performing the preflight checks. But evidently they did not check the flight controls for correctness of movement. The twin roared down the runway, lifted off and rolled over, cartwheeling and bursting into flames. Both pilots died.

NTSB investigators examined the wreckage and were able to determine that the left aileron was connected backwards. While the status of the cables in the right wing was not confirmed due to fire damage, the misconnection that was discovered could have caused both ailerons to be deflected upward when the wheel was turned either way. If the pilots had checked to see that the ailerons were moving properly, they would likely be alive today.

External gust locks are a great idea, especially on rudders; don't forget to remove them before flight.

Locked Up Tight

It's surprising how many pilots manage to make it out to the runway and start the takeoff without ever trying to move the controls at all. It's even more surprising for them when they discover the control locks still in place.

One pilot started his takeoff in a Cessna 182 with a gust lock in the yoke. As the plane gathered speed, he realized what was happening and tried to remove the lock from the column; but before he could get it out, the Cessna ran off the runway and flipped on its back, seriously injuring the pilot. The control lock did come out—after the yoke broke at the lock holes.

Another pilot managed to get his Cessna 150 off the ground even though an external gust lock was holding the ailerons in place. He even managed to get around the pattern, but he couldn't manage a landing, and the aircraft was destroyed when it ran off the side of the runway and through a wire fence.

Sometimes, controls lock up for other reasons. The pilot of a chartered Piper Navajo might have saved himself and his passengers from harm if he had checked the controls for free and proper movement before takeoff, or if he had taken a close look at the tail area during preflight. Witnesses watched the Navajo accelerate down the runway at Prescott, Arizona, and lift into a very nose-high attitude. It stalled and fell back to the runway, seriously injuring all ten persons aboard. The NTSB investigation found the elevator stop bolts had backed out eight threads and would not permit full nose-down travel of the elevators.

On this and many other aircraft, the stop bolts are plainly visible by looking through the openings at the base of the rudder. Many pilots check that the bolts are present, but how many take note of the number of threads which should be visible? At the very least, pilots should check these bolts periodically for security.

Check, Please

The unschooled nature of many pilots' preflight inspections was illustrated dramatically a few years ago in a demonstration staged by the British Civil Aviation Authority at a fly-in. In a test of preflight scrutiny, the CAA set up a Beagle Pup single-engine trainer with 11 "planted" defects. Pilots were invited to preflight the aircraft and list the discrepancies they found.

Defects included no exhaust pipe (it had been removed), a large amount of water in the right fuel tank, brake fluid seeping from a line, and others, all with the potential of causing a serious accident.

To the surprise of many, only one pilot of the 58 who participated found all 11 defects. Only six pilots found ten defects, while 15 found nine defects. Most surprising was that more than half of the participants did not find the water-contaminated fuel. Many did not bother to use the fuel-sampling bottles in plain sight nearby.

The British exercise demonstrated the deadly implications of failure to perform what might be termed a "normal" preflight. For true peace of mind, a pilot might resolve to make the extra effort, getting into the habit of performing a "super-normal" preflight. For pilots who are truly concerned with fire prevention rather than fire fighting, preflighting with that extra attention to detail can be the difference between a pleasant flight and disaster.

Quality Control on Preflight

When considered in industrial terms, a preflight inspection is really a quality control project. The pilot surveys the product in order to determine if everything meets some predetermined standards for fit, function, operation of the components, etc.

Just as singers and dancers have style, so do inspectors. Using a standardized test, two researchers classified people as being either reflectives (long time to judge, make few errors), impulsives (short time, more errors), fast-accurates (short time, few errors), or slow-inaccurates (long time, more errors). Then they set out to see what those styles meant in terms of inspection errors.

The inspection task consisted of deciding whether a particular character existed among a field of other characters projected on a screen, and then deciding if the "flaw" character met certain size criteria that would allow it to be recorded as a "pass."

Those who rated as reflectives and fast-accurates on the standardized test were significantly faster in detecting certain flaws, and they made fewer size-judgment errors. That might appear both obvious and desirable; but what's less obvious, and perhaps more important to pilots, is that the "inaccurates" actually detected more flaws than the "accurates." That is, there were fewer instances in which they failed to note the appearance of a flaw.

While industrial inspection is a trade-off between speed (and thus economics) and quality, zero-defect inspection is more properly the goal of the pilot whose safety can depend on the absolute accuracy of the preflight inspection. Perhaps pilots will one day be tested for their inspection style as part of the training regimen.

Am I Forgetting Something?

Even though draining the fuel tank sumps is one of the first things a student pilot is taught, water in the fuel brings down airplanes with surprising regularity. Students are cautioned about the possibility of condensation forming in partially filled tanks, but in reality more water comes from poorly maintained or designed filler caps and fuel systems than from condensation. In any case, the only way to be certain the engine will be getting fuel instead of water is to make a sump check a part of every preflight. Some pilots never even bother with the sump drains at all, and they eventually rust shut.

Failure to drain the sumps led to the crash of a Piper Arrow III in Oklawaha, Florida. According to the pilot's wife, a passenger who survived the accident, he had the airplane refueled the night before and had drained the engine fuel strainer, but not the tank sumps. At 7:20 on the morning of the crash, the flight departed Fort Lauderdale and continued normally until near Lake Kissimmee. At that point, the pilot switched from the right to the left tank, and the engine began to run rough. A call was immediately made to Orlando Approach Control, and the pilot declared an emergency. After making the call, he switched back to the right tank, and the engine resumed normal operation.

The Orlando controller informed him that he was 50 miles from Leesburg (his planned intermediate stop) and that the nearest airport was at Kissimmee, ten miles away. The pilot elected to make a precautionary landing at Kissimmee. Vectors were issued, and he landed uneventfully.

Once on the ground, he taxied the Arrow to the ramp, but did not shut down the engine. According to a statement by his wife, he switched tanks and ran up the engine several times, with no unusual roughness noticed. She then got out of the airplane, removed the left fuel cap and checked the fuel level in the tank, noting that it was full. Interestingly, witnesses observed she had a fuel sampler/screwdriver in her hand, but did not use it to drain fuel.

The Piper stayed on the ground for another 10 to 15 minutes, then departed. The pilot never got out of the airplane.

The pilot circled Kissimmee for a short time, then proceeded north. He decided not to land at Leesburg, continuing instead to the final destination, a private airport a few miles northeast of Oklawaha. Witnesses at the airport said that the Arrow passed over the airport heading northwest at about 300 feet AGL, continuing on for a quarter of a mile before descending out of sight. The witnesses heard the engine lose power just before the descent, then heard the sound of a crash shortly after.

When they reached the crash site, witnesses found the pilot dead and his wife trapped in the wreckage. No odor of fuel was noted, and there was no fire.

The Arrow had struck a large pine tree and broken into several pieces, strewing wreckage in a line starting about 150 yards from the tree. The right wing broke in two pieces, and separated from the fuselage. The left wing broke at the root, and the engine and propeller separated from the front of the airplane. The fuselage and tail came to rest inverted.

Examination of the wreckage revealed that the right tank, which was intact, had no fuel in it (and none near it on the ground), and the left tank, which was ruptured, contained about 1.5 gallons. The fuel selector was found between the Left and Off positions (the Piper's fuel selector is located on the left side wall of the cockpit, with the Off position straight back, Left pointing up, and Right pointing forward—there's also a lock between the Left and Off positions). The electric boost pump was on. The gear and flaps were extended. The propeller, which was still attached to the engine, showed very little chordwise scratching, indicating that it was not turning at the time of impact.

A partial teardown of the engine showed that there was nothing but water in the engine-driven fuel pump, the fuel injector divider block, and the fuel control filter. A small amount of fuel was found in the line between the electric fuel pump and the fuel control filter.

The main sump drains were removed and inspected. They were both corroded to the point they had to be forced open, indicating that they had rarely—if ever—been used.

Other Liquid Concerns

Checking fuel quality during a preflight inspection ranks right up there as one of the most important things a pilot must do before venturing into the air. Also near the top of the "must do" list is a check of oil quantity; an aircraft engine—even a very small one—will only run so long without lubrication.

An Arizona flight instructor ferried a student to an airport in a Cessna 150. It had been a short flight, taking less than an hour, and the turn-around was equally quick; in short order the CFI was preparing to depart for home.

The Cessna had been topped off with oil that very morning, and the dipstick showed full, the instructor remembered. There was really no reason to worry about the oil. But something made him check the dipstick once more. The level was down about two quarts. At that rate of consumption, the engine might have been in serious jeopardy by the time the plane arrived near home base. (The C-150 engine has a six-quart oil capacity, and Continental warns not to operate it with less than four quarts.)

"Now," he said, "I check the oil level every time before I fire up. If it happened that one time, it'll happen again."

The true value of extra-effort preflight inspections does not always show up in the accident statistics. Rather, it is found in the accidents that don't happen, the saves made before the aircraft ever leaves the tiedown by pilots who looked a little harder and a little closer.

But every now and then, we come across a preflight situation over which the pilot has almost no control, and in which an unreasonably detailed inspection would have been required to disclose the problem. Of course, the unexpected power failures are the ones we train for.

A pilot and his father had taken off from an Iowa airport for a short flight, and as the Cherokee passed through 150 feet, the engine quit. The pilot tried to land on a road, but couldn't quite make it, and the airplane crashed.

After the accident, the pilot wrote a simple, one-sentence statement to investigators: "Mouse nest in air intake box plugged carburetor airflow at approximately 150 feet after takeoff."

FAA inspectors examined the Cherokee and found the mouse nest lodged in the carburetor throat. They also found another such nest behind the magnetos. The inspectors said that the nest in the carburetor airbox would have been impossible for the pilot to detect during preflight without disassembling the induction system. They also stated they believed the nest had held in place during taxi and the takeoff roll, then came loose and clogged the carburetor.

Painstaking Preflights Prevent Painful Discoveries

Recently back from some major airframe work, the Cessna 421B was sporting new paint and a new set of elevators. The pilot, a 9,590-hour ATP, was preparing to conduct a test flight to check the airplane's radios and autopilot in preparation for the twin's sale later in the month.

> After departing Tucson International Airport, the pilot and a young passenger "along for the ride" had flown about 14 miles to nearby Ryan Field for some touch-and-goes.
>
> Witnesses near the field told of watching the Cessna do about six touch-and-goes, all of which appeared normal in every respect. But as the airplane turned onto the downwind leg, it pitched sharply downward, made three turns, crashed and exploded. Both occupants were killed.
>
> Investigation showed that the elevators had been installed without any balance weights, and the tail surfaces fluttered to the point of snapping the rivets on the elevator push-pull tubes, pitching the aircraft out of control.

Could this pilot have saved himself before leaving the ground? Was he doomed by an inadequate preflight? Were the missing balance weights hidden flaws, or were they merely hidden by the pilot's preflight habits?

"Inadequate preflight preparation and planning" by the pilot in command is cited by the NTSB as the primary probable cause in about 12 percent of all accidents (in a typical year, there were 412 such cases out of 3,502 total crashes). However, since the NTSB lumps several common types of probable cause statements into the same computer bin (failure to check weather, miscalculation of aircraft range, etc.), the category is somewhat over inflated. Nonetheless, the pilot's failure to conduct a proper and thorough preflight inspection accounts for a major share of accidents.

Obviously, the responsibility for prevention of these accidents lies with the pilot. Noticing a loose fuel cap, finding water in the fuel, spotting a damaged wingtip are all things which conscientious pilots should find before takeoff.

That's a "normal" preflight. But there are things beyond what is normally considered to be part of the preflight which, with a little extra effort or a little more attention to details, could be caught before leaving the ground. The pilot who catches these items is often rewarded by the knowledge that he probably saved his own life and those of his passengers.

In the Cessna 421 case, the missing balance weights would have been apparent in a mere glance at the elevators during preflight. But it may have been that the pilot looked at the elevators without really seeing what was there. Too often, pilots look for obvious things like hinge bolts and nuts, but look no further. This is particularly true of items which require a little extra effort or vigilance to detect potential problems.

Another case in point involved a Piper Arrow flying over the desert at night. The pilot suddenly discovered an electrical fire. Turning off the master switch did not help, and he found to his dismay that the radios and lights kept on working even with the master off. The fire kept going, too.

Immediately following this, the elevator failed to respond to his control inputs, and he was forced to land the aircraft in a lake bed using the throttle for pitch control.

Investigators found that the battery, located in the tail of the Arrow, had come out of its box and bounced around, arcing against the control cables and starting the fire. Then it cut through the cables, rendering the elevator and rudder useless.

It's arguable that most pilots would have been caught in the same predicament. The Arrow's battery box is situated behind a panel in the aft baggage area. Its lid is held on with four camlock fasteners, and some maintenance personnel are not careful enough to engage the fasteners; other times, wear and tear makes it possible for vibration to unlatch them.

But the Arrow pilot who really wants to assure himself of absolute safety should remove the access panel and look into the tailcone at the battery box prior to each flight. It may be a case of "too careful" preflighting, but it's far better than the alternative.

The 25-Cent Inspection

Preflight inspections are no longer the cursory affairs they once were. Merely kicking the tires and starting the engine is not enough for many aircraft. Pilots must now poke and prod, shake, twist and tweak various components to be sure they're attached and functioning properly.

But whereas preflight inspections used to involve primarily the hands and eyes of the pilot, hearing is growing to become more and more an integral part of the preflight. And this might lead to one of the cheapest inspections ever—the 25-cent inspection.

Years ago, it became a part of every Grumman AA-1 and AA-5 pilot's routine to take a quarter and tap on the control surface bonding lines. A change in the sound of the tap indicated possible delamination or debonding of the control surface skin.

More recently, owners of Piper Malibus may have been looking for mechanics with a tool box full of quarters for an inspection of the bonded prop spinner on that airplane. One series of spinners on the Malibu contains domes with an internal bulkhead bonded with adhesive. After some time in service, it was found that some of these spinners may have been bonded inadequately, resulting in separation of the forward support bulkhead. This could lead to eventual spinner dome failure.

The inspection, which must be done by a qualified A&P, calls for removal of the spinner, then a close look at the bond between the inner dome surface and the rear edge of the internal dome support bulkhead. Debonding might be detected by eye along this seam. If it is, the spinner goes back to the factory for repairs. If not, then it's time for the next step.

Failing to detect any debonding by eye, the mechanic now moves on to a dye-penetrant inspection of the bond line. This inspection calls for a non-fluorescent dye penetrant, and if definite debonding is found, the spinner goes back to the factory for repairs. However, if debonding is suspected, but not proved by the dye-penetrant inspection, the final powers of the mechanic are called into play—he must use his ears.

The spinner manufacturer calls this step the "tap test." A steel washer slightly larger than a quarter is used to tap along the bonding line inside the spinner dome support bulkhead. The mechanic should be listening for "a dull clunking," which indicates debonding; areas still holding together will give a good, sharp rapping sound. Again, if debonding is found, the spinner goes back to the factory for repairs.

The 25-cent inspection isn't limited to Grummans and Malibu prop spinners. Any aircraft using glue, fiberglass, or composites is a good candidate for the aural test. For example, pilots can keep an ear on the condition of a fiberglass wingtip by giving it a going over with a quarter once in a while. Areas where the sound changes might indicate delamination of the material. Fiberglass radomes also respond to this test.

In particular, experts say, pilots should focus on bonding lines and attach points—like rivet, screw, or fastener lines—when looking for problems. Any changes in the sound produced by tapping may indicate potential trouble, and a closer examination is in order.

Loading Considerations

Sir Hiram Maxim, scientist and inventor of the late 19th century, dreamed up things in very large dimensions. In addition to his machine gun, an invention that fired very large numbers of bullets, Sir Hiram dabbled in aviation, and conceived a very large biplane, whose 4,000 square-foot double wings measured 110 feet from tip to tip. Two steam engines (yep, steam engines!) of 180 horsepower each were connected to a pair of propellers nearly 18 feet in diameter. All up, including a crew of three, the Maxim flying machine weighed 7,000 pounds.

That's a lot of airplane for 360 horsepower, but the inventor had great confidence, so great in fact that on the first full-blown test flight in 1894 the Maxim monster was mounted on rails to keep it from rising more than a few inches. And rise a bit it did, but the almost total lack of control caused it to bind on one of the rails, the airplane was badly damaged, and no further tests were attempted. Another pre-Wright brothers try that failed.

Even if the Maxim airplane had been invested with adequate control, it probably wouldn't have flown very far or very high because of the excessive power loading; each one of those steam-powered horses was responsible for 19.5 pounds of airplane. (By comparison, a Piper Seminole, with two equally powerful engines, has a power loading of 10.6 pounds per horsepower.)

But that was a more imaginative age, and airplane designer-builders had absolutely no guidelines when it came to how much an airplane should weigh—bigger was almost always considered

A computer capable of doing weight and balance computations helps the pilot keep the aircraft below gross and within its center of gravity envelope.

to be better. But the certification rules that have governed aircraft design for decades limit weight by requiring minimum performance; an airplane with whatever power is installed must be able to climb at a certain rate, or the maximum weight is lowered. There are of course other parameters of design that impact the total number of pounds allowable, but when an airplane is finally certificated, its performance is based primarily on weight.

Fortunately, weight is probably the easiest thing for a pilot to control. There's no rule that says you must always take off with the fuel tanks filled, or the baggage compartments stuffed with luggage, or passengers in all the seats. Takeoff weight (and therefore landing weight) can be adjusted to meet the needs of the mission, one of which is to stay within the operating limitations imposed on the airplane.

Aircraft loading is usually addressed as a dual subject—weight, and balance—and we see no good reason to depart from that tradition. The two are inseparable, and together can have a significant negative effect on performance. A very heavy airplane is one thing, but a very heavy airplane with a center of gravity located beyond the limits may exhibit performance and handling characteristics that no pilot can handle. With that in mind, then, let's look at weight first.

More Than One Kind of Weight

First, there's *empty weight.* It will be different for each and every airplane, because no matter how hard they try to standardize their product, manufacturers simply cannot make each unit come off the assembly line an exact copy of the one that went before. The larger the airplane, the greater the disparity is likely to be. We're not talking about huge differences here, but in order to comply with the limitations, a pilot needs to know the exact empty weight; it's the foundation of all weight and balance calculations. (Airline operators modify this slightly and use a figure known as *basic operating weight,* which is empty weight plus all the things that would normally be on board when the airplane is ready to accept passengers, baggage, cargo and fuel. Included in basic operating weight are crewmembers and their equipment, food, beverages and other standard necessities.)

For most small airplanes, the next limitation is *maximum takeoff weight.* It's a combination of structural and performance considerations, and it will be exactly the same figure for each unit in a particular model designation (i.e., for each Cessna 172, each Piper Cherokee, each Beech Baron, and so on.) When the landing gear can stand it, some manufacturers add a few pounds to account for the fuel that will be consumed during taxiing and engine runup; the resultant figure is called *ramp weight,* or *taxi weight.*

Between empty weight and maximum takeoff weight are the pounds accounted for by occupants, baggage/cargo and fuel. This will obviously vary from one plane to the next because empty weights are all somewhat different, but this figure has found a niche as a marketing tool. It's usually referred to as *useful load,* and represents a fair indication of an airplane's capabilities in the toting department.

Within limits, a pilot can load some of each, or a lot of one and none of another as the upcoming flight requires. There's a lot of flexibility in the quantity and distribution of useful load.

Even though the pilot had been cautioned that the Piper Cherokee 140 he was renting would not legally carry full fuel plus four occupants, that was approximately the loading condition it was in when it crashed into an apartment building at Bowling Green, Ohio, killing everyone aboard. No one else was injured, but the resulting fire caused a total loss of the apartment building, which was being used as a university dormitory.

The pilot was a young man who had obtained his private pilot certificate only five months earlier and was believed to have about 100 hours of flying time. He arranged to rent the Cherokee the day before the crash and at that time, he was told he could not load the airplane full of people and fuel, as he intended. The FBO sensed that some education was in order, and suggested that the pilot work out a weight and balance calculation to demonstrate the loading limitations. The NTSB investigator obtained a copy of a weight and balance calculation in the pilot's handwriting. It showed four people averaging 155 pounds each, plus 40 pounds of baggage, which pushed the airplane's weight to within 75 pounds of its maximum gross weight, without any fuel on board.

The "top 'em off" syndrome may have been working actively during the preflight preparations, because the Cherokee was nearly full of fuel when the pilot took off with two other young men as passengers. Perhaps he thought that the trip to Bowling Green would burn enough fuel to offset the over-gross condition; but how much fuel can a Cherokee 140 consume on a 20-mile flight?

The takeoff was apparently uneventful, as was the trip to Bowling Green, but here the pilot laid on the straw that broke the Cherokee's back—he picked up yet another passenger, and the total weight must have been very close to the calculation the day before that showed the airplane loaded beyond its limits.

Single-engine airplanes are capable of rather awesome feats of load-carrying. For example, when Max Conrad was setting long-distance records years ago, his Piper Comanche got off the ground at incredible weights...but Max selected very long runways with clear zones at the departure ends. Given enough runway, even a low-powered airplane can eventually accelerate to an airspeed that will lift the load.

This pilot didn't have that luxury; Runway 24 at the Bowling Green Airport is only 3,000 feet long. It aims a pilot directly toward the campus of Bowling Green State University and a wall of multi-story buildings; not only is a reasonable climb required, but a pilot must turn shortly after takeoff.

The Cherokee never gained more than about 50 feet of altitude according to eyewitnesses, who also noticed a lot of yawing and wing-rocking right up to the point of impact, about a quarter-mile off the end of the runway. The occupants didn't stand a chance—the Cherokee was crash-bound from the instant the pilot elected to continue an impossible takeoff.

Flying Safely With No Fuel

As airplane cabins grew to accommodate more weight over the years, a dilemma began to develop in the structural strength department. The increased weight expressed itself on the wing spars, which are always trying to bend upwards as lift is produced. The designers had to do one of two things; make the wing spars stronger (which in itself increases weight even more) or limit the number of pounds that might be loaded in the cabin. Both solutions are evident in various models in the fleet, but designers who chose the weight-limiting route created one of the most confusing terms in the business—*zero-fuel weight.*

Imagine an airplane with wing spars strong enough to carry 3,000 pounds without breaking; add one more pound at the center of the wing (where the bending force is expressed) in flight and...snap! The bending force created by lift can be cut down somewhat by the weight of fuel in wing tanks, but what if you find yourself running on the fumes some day? Or, how about getting the tanks close to empty and encountering turbulence that generates a couple of Gs? The 3,000-pound load on the wing spar suddenly becomes 4,500 pounds, and that may be enough to break the wing. Even though this airplane might have a maximum gross weight of 4,000 pounds, you would be limited to not more than 3,000 pounds in the cabin; any weight above that figure would have to be in the form of fuel in the wing tanks in order to respect the breaking point of the spars.

An airplane whose limitations include a zero-fuel weight must be considered in a different light when loading time comes around. You need to know the difference between empty weight and zero-fuel weight; that's the number of pounds of stuff—people or things, take your choice—you can safely put in the cabin, and it's a number that won't change. It will affect your loading decisions when you need to fill the seats and the baggage compartments; develop a set of working numbers for your airplane and when it appears it's going to be close to the limit, make a careful calculation of the actual numbers. Remember that a zero-fuel weight limitation puts an absolute ceiling on the number of people and the amount of baggage that can be loaded.

> Here's a quick test. The airplane you are preparing to fly has an empty weight of 4,000 pounds, a maximum takeoff weight of 6,000 pounds, fuel tanks that hold 1,200 pounds, and a zero-fuel weight limit of 5,000 pounds. Your trip requires 700 pounds of fuel. How many pounds of passengers and baggage may be loaded?
>
> The answer is 1,000 pounds, period—that's for today, tomorrow, or any time this airplane is flown, and has nothing to do with how much fuel you need for the trip. When you load 1,000 pounds of people or things, you have reached the zero-fuel weight limit, and all weight beyond that point must be in the form of fuel.

More Fuel, More Problems

Fuel for most of the two- and four-seat airplanes in the general aviation fleet is almost traditional—"top 'em off." Not only does a full fuel load seldom come close to over-grossing the airplane, the range is often severely compromised with less than full tanks, and we've been carefully taught that filling the tanks after every flight helps avoid fuel contamination from condensation. There's one more factor driving the "full tanks" theory. Light-airplane fuel gauges are notorious for their unreliability, and the only way a pilot *really* knows what's in the tanks is when they are filled.

We're not picking on Cherokee 140s, but they have been involved in a number of takeoff-performance accidents. Do pilots have a false sense of capability because of the size and seating arrangement of this airplane?

A failed takeoff attempt from the Sierra Blanca Airport in Ruidoso, New Mexico, resulted in injuries to a Cherokee pilot and his two passengers. The airplane was substantially damaged when it crashed just beyond the airport perimeter. Investigators said the 199-hour pilot had flown to Ruidoso earlier in the day to pick up a passenger and return to Fort Worth, Texas. After landing at the 6,810-foot elevation airport, he had performed some weight and balance calculations for the return trip. Based on these calculations, and believing that the left tank was empty, he requested that only the right fuel tank be filled.

But during the preflight, the pilot discovered that the left tank was full, so he recalculated the airplane's weight, and later told investigators, "my self-imposed safety margin had been used up by the extra fuel." His calculations showed he was still under the maximum gross weight, so he did not pursue the matter of the unwanted fuel.

Having loaded 46 pounds of baggage, a 120-pound passenger in the rear seat, a 200-pound passenger in the right front seat, and his own 240 pounds in the left front seat, the pilot taxied for takeoff. He told investigators that the runup was normal, and after taking runway, he ran it up to full power with the brakes locked, leaning the mixture to obtain maximum rpm.

After liftoff and a climb to 150 feet AGL (the Cherokee was now struggling at an altitude near 7,000 feet) the pilot encountered turbulence, another of Mother Nature's performance thieves, and the airplane began to sink. He pulled the nose up to obtain the best angle of climb speed in an attempt to arrest the descent, but the plane continued to sink toward a road beyond the airport boundary.

As he approached the road, he pulled the nose up farther, trying to zoom, and the Cherokee cleared the road, but crashed in a field just beyond. That was the pilot's story.

The tower operator witnessed most of the action and gave investigators a somewhat different account. He said the Cherokee lifted off and climbed a bit, then assumed a very nose-high attitude and started to sink. The controller thought it would land back on the runway, but the pilot put the nose down and recovered.

The Cherokee started climbing again, but as it did, the pilot pulled the nose up again and predictably, the Cherokee started sinking. The tower operator stated it "looked like he'd crash." But the pilot lowered the nose and recovered again. Finally, he pulled the nose up for a third time and sank out of sight beyond the perimeter trees. The controller saw a cloud of dust and knew the Cherokee had crashed.

Post-accident investigation revealed that both tanks on the Cherokee were indeed full. The right tank had been filled to the filler tab, but the left tank was found full of autogas. Apparently it had been filled at some other location, because the fuel receipt from Sierra Blanca showed that only 21 gallons of avgas had been delivered.

Investigators believe the Cherokee was over its maximum gross weight. It's interesting to note that in his accident report, the pilot identified the airplane as a Piper PA-28-150. This model has a maximum gross weight of 2,150 pounds, versus the PA-28-140, which in some models can have a maximum weight of as little as 1,950 pounds. But even that slip-up wouldn't have made any difference; the airplane would have been overweight regardless of its designation, according to handbook information.

Stepping up through the ranks of complexity, the large singles and the light twins represent a class of airplane that can be overloaded by topping the tanks. These airplanes are characterized by roomy cabins, big luggage compartments, and long legs...enough fuel capacity to take large groups of people to interesting places far away, with the attendant luggage, sports equipment, and so on. And at the other end of the trip, with the trophies of hunting, fishing and shopping sprees already loaded, there's a strong temptation to fill the tanks and make it all the way home without a fuel stop. If that much fuel drives the takeoff weight beyond the limit, there may be trouble ahead. Never load an airplane beyond its limits; there's nothing magic about full tanks.

Maximum landing weight must also be considered in the loading process, and it's obviously a structural limit. The wheels, gear struts, attach points and other components are designed to absorb the stresses of a normal landing (whatever *that* is!) plus a fudge factor, and beyond that, structural failure. A very hard landing could do the job, as could a "normal" touchdown at a weight in excess of the limit. It all boils down to the amount of energy expended when the wheels touch the runway; it's a combination of weight and vertical speed—increase either, or both, and the results might be very damaging.

Sometimes it's difficult to figure out whether an accident is the result of trying to continue a takeoff or attempt a landing. Either way, this Alaskan helicopter pilot paid the price for overloading.

This commercial pilot was no beginner; he had 7,700 hours of pilot time, and 5,000 hours in the Hughes 369 helicopter. He had flown from Petersburg to Woedeski Island earlier in the day, intending to bring back four geologists and their equipment.

The pilot was aware that the chopper was at or possibly above its maximum allowable gross weight when he attempted to take off. He said that on his first try, the chopper lifted but the low rotor-speed warning light came on and he put it back down. Helicopter pilots have a big advantage over their fixed-wing brethren in that they can make a short vertical "trial run" without hazard; it's a matter of applying all the power that the engine can develop and seeing if the aircraft will leave the ground. If it won't, so be it; but if it will, ground effect is probably at work, and once the aircraft moves "off the bubble," there may not be enough lift to sustain flight. A warning of low rotor speed would mean that the angle of attack necessary to overcome the helicopter's weight was slowing the rotor, and the warning flags should be flying—the prospects for a successful takeoff were not good.

But the pilot was not to be denied, and attempted a second takeoff, only to have the low rotor-speed warning come on again. Finally, he made a third attempt, during which the chopper struggled to about 20 feet above the

				+700	128.04 % M.A.C.		610502
SIC EMPTY AIRPLANE TH FULL OIL 22 QTS. ➡				4809	127.60 % M.A.C.		613678

COLUMN 1					COLUMN 2			
TEMS WEIGHED BUT NOT PART F BASIC WEIGHT	WEIGHT	ARM	MOMENT		BASIC ITEMS NOT IN AIRPLANE WHEN WEIGHED	WEIGHT	ARM	MOME
JEL @ 5.83 ./GAL.					8 life jackets	4	137.0	5
112 GALS.	653	126.8	82795					
UNUSABLE	27	129	3483					
80 GALS.	466	148.0	69027					
UNUSABLE	24	148	3552					
USABLE FUEL	1068	135.5	144788					
	0	0.0	0					
	0	0.0	0					
TOTAL	0	0.0	0		TOTAL	4	137.0	5
ACTIONS USED:					ELECTRONIC WEIGHING KIT TYPE: C-55800-3-5			

Multi-engine aircraft used in for-hire service must be weighed every 36 months, a procedure that must be done very carefully if the resulting data is to be useful.

ground, but was unable to clear a line of 30-foot trees about 50 feet from the takeoff point. The helicopter hit the ground and rolled over.

FAA inspectors examined the wreckage and found nothing mechanically amiss. The passengers were transported to the nearby airport and weighed. When all the weights were totaled up, it was found that the helicopter was 200 pounds heavier than its maximum allowable weight.

You've Gotta Land Sometime

Most singles and many light twins are designed so that they may be safely landed immediately following a maximum-weight takeoff; but there are a few of these airplanes with landing-weight limits, and it's the pilot's responsibility to check the book and be sure. If you find yourself at the wheel of such an airplane and it becomes absolutely imperative that you return to earth right after takeoff, you've two choices—fly around until enough fuel is con-

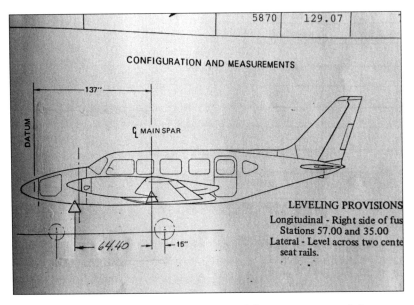

Aircraft weighing reports include detailed data on empty weight, arms and the center of gravity envelope. The method of weighing is specified in the report.

sumed to reduce airplane weight to the landing limit, or make the smoothest landing of your career. If the problem happens to be engine failure, the single-engine pilot's decision is made; the multi-engine pilot must consider all the factors bearing on the situation and do what appears best at the time. (Turbine-powered airplanes must carry large amounts of fuel because of the much higher consumption rate of jet engines. As a result, most of them have landing weights hundreds, sometimes thousands of pounds below maximum takeoff weights. The dilemma is resolved through the use of fuel-dumping systems that can get rid of a lot of pounds in a hurry in an emergency. Another good reason to avoid the area below and behind a heavy jet on takeoff!)

Be alert to this situation: You're faced with a short trip in an airplane with a heavy load, full tanks and a landing-weight limit; if the planned fuel consumption will not reduce the weight to the landing limit, you'll have to defuel. Better yet, make it a habit to avoid fueling such an airplane until all the votes are in—passenger and baggage weight, minimum fuel requirements and so on. It's a lot easier—and less expensive—to call for a specific fuel load at the last minute than it is to defuel the airplane.

Fuel and Center of Gravity

It's probably a very fortuitous thing that the airplanes most likely to be topped off for each flight (i.e., most of the singles) are also designed so that the fuel tanks are at or near the center of gravity, and the CG doesn't change very much as fuel is consumed in flight. That particular problem is usually reserved for larger airplanes, and invests the pilot with an additional responsibility—making sure that the CG for landing is within limits.

There's a quick way to check an airplane for this characteristic: If the weight-and-balance section of the handbook lists only one moment arm for fuel, you can rest assured that the CG won't change significantly as gasoline is burned. But when the loading charts indicate a different moment arm for every ten gallons or so of fuel, you will probably need to calculate the landing CG location for a long trip to be absolutely certain you'll have full control when you slow down for landing.

The Other Loading Problem: Weight Distribution

A pilot's loading calculations are only as good as the data on which they're based. Veteran flight-test pilot Bill Kelly shares his thoughts on some of the problems associated with "bad paperwork," and reviews the process of weighing and balancing an airplane properly:

Several years ago I signed on to do some flight tests related to the crash investigation of an old Navajo. We rented one of the crashed Navajo's siblings—also very old. Our test bed seemed to have a very complete paperwork record—many 337s detailing various configuration changes; new radios exchanged for old, new interior, stereo, potty seat, refreshment center, etc. Each of the modifications included a revised basic empty weight and CG calculation, or the words "Weight and CG change negligible." There had even been two other weighings over the many years since the airplane was built.

The crash had occurred with the plane full of people, and near its gross weight and aft CG limits. Rather than use real live people to bring our tests up to weight, I had used a pile of 40-pound bags of Sacrete. All this was carefully loaded and tied down, to simulate the loading of the crashed Navajo. The latest revised basic empty weight and CG data was used to determine the ballast location. After careful checks of engine timing, cylinder compression, control and trim travels, we were ready to fly.

That first test flight was eye-opening, to say the least. No longitudinal stability at all, and absolutely no climb performance with one engine running at "zero thrust" to simulate a dead and feathered powerplant. Something was seriously wrong—Navajos don't fly like that when loaded within limits.

The next stop was an FBO with a set of certified aircraft scales, then a trip to the hardware store to get a chalk line, tape measure, and plumb bob. The ballast was unloaded, and fuel tanks filled. Then a real careful weighing, plus accurate measurement of mainwheel-to-datum and nosewheel-to-datum distances—all this after a meticulous leveling of the airplane as it sat on the scales.

The results? After subtracting out the fuel weight, this old bird was several hundred pounds heavier, and two inches more tail heavy than what showed on the last weight and CG sheet! We reloaded the ballast using the new data, and had an airplane that flew like a Navajo should.

But what if that first test flight had been a real passenger-carrying flight, maybe on a dark night into instrument conditions, and with a lot of turbulence? Or maybe from a field at high density altitude? Or with an engine failure shortly after takeoff?

I never could figure out the big mistake in the Navajo's paperwork. All of the arithmetic worked out, but a lot of equipment had been removed or installed over the years, and I had no way of verifying the actual weight or moment arm of each piece. And of course I had no way of checking the accuracy of the scales that had been used in the previous weighings.

There are lots of 20- to 50-year-old airplanes out there that haven't been weighed since they left the factory, but in their lifetimes have seen several repaint jobs, re-fabrics, major repairs, new interiors, radios and instruments. Lots of the younger planes have also had much equipment replacement. There's nothing wrong with "calculating" a revised weight and CG following modifications, but the final answer is only as good as the previous basic empty weight and CG. When in doubt—get a new weighing.

A "weighing" is one procedure that I would want to watch—to be sure it was done properly. There are good weighings, and bad weighings—and a bad one is worse than no weighing at all. And a weighing on good scales *without* accurate measurement of moment arms is meaningless—you will get a perfect reading of weight but have a possibly horribly erroneous CG position.

Section Six of the newer GAMA-style Approved Flight Manuals (AFM), plus the Service Manual usually provide a detailed procedure for the weighing. The Type Certificate Data Sheet (in your FBO's fiche machine) also gives some data on leveling means, datum location, etc. Beware of the shop that just shoves the plane onto the scales, reads the three weights, then pulls the plane back out of the hangar.

The Cheyenne AFM nicely states all of the necessary wheel centerline measurements from datum, but you have to read the fine print to discover that the oleos must be blocked in the fully-extended position for these measurements to be valid. Some of the Beeches have forward-slanting main struts, and main wheel-to-datum will vary with strut extension. The Cessna T210 manual calls for stringing a line between the main axles, then measuring from this line to a plumb dropped from the firewall datum to get the main wheel moment arm.

From my experience, taildraggers should always be measured. The main gear centerlines can vary considerably between airplanes—and from the example in the manual. The tailwheel measurement is especially critical since any slight change in leaf spring length or curvature, or swapping between Maule and Scott wheel assemblies, may make a significant change in the tailwheel-to-datum measurement.

When in doubt—measure. Use a plumb bob to drop really vertical lines, and be sure to measure in the horizontal. A chalk line on a clean hangar floor is a big aid in assuring that all measures are parallel to the centerline. And don't bother weighing or measuring until the airplane is absolutely level—"un-level" screws up both the scale readings and the longitudinal tape measurements.

Beware of "bathroom" scales: Some of them are real accurate, but my experience has been that the poundage displayed may vary with the location of the weight on the small platform. I sometimes use such scales, but only after calibrating them with known weights, and when I'm sure I can locate the tailwheel precisely on-center. However, a slight error of one or two pounds on such scales might be preferable to using a 20,000 pound scale where you can't read the results to closer than within ten pounds.

The real test of airplane weighing and subsequent weight and CG calculations comes with the homebuilt "slicks" and vintage ragwing taildraggers. With the homebuilts there are a lot of variables from what the kit designer originally intended. Like where is that full-length wet leading edge gas tank really located? Or is the pilot's fanny really at 60 inches behind the datum like the plans show? What about that super-soft upholstery on that re-clined plastic seat bucket—did it move the fanny arm forward? The same problems appear with that restored Piper Pacer or Cessna 170, with their extra fuel tanks, modern panels full of state-of-the-art avionics, wheel axle extensions, and plush interior upholstery.

Before we get into a sample problem, let's discuss that elusive "Datum," sometimes known as "Station Zero." A datum is simply a reference point, usually a fixed distance from some hard, immovable point like a wing leading edge. A few single-engine machines still use the firewall or leading edge for a datum. This is a little confusing if you start making changes in the engine compartment, or if your bird only comes with a real "empty" weight—now you will have to add in positive pounds of oil on every loading, at a negative arm and get a resulting negative moment to be subtracted from the total for the people, baggage, and fuel moments.

The best place for a "datum" is about a foot ahead of the tip of the prop spinner or radome. Now all arms will have a (+) sign, and all weight additions will give a positive moment. In fact, if you don't like your datum location, move it. If it's at the firewall, just move it ahead five feet, then add 60 inches to all other important stations, such as seats, fuel and baggage.

Now let's work a problem, using a high-wing taildragger for our example. To make the problem harder, it's a garage-factory special, built from plans. The builder has made a few modifications to the side-by-side seating, and has installed wing fuel tanks in lieu of the fuselage tank. Make sure the airplane is carefully leveled on the scales, and with plumb lines dropped from the datum, main axles, and tailwheel axle. (If the scales get in the way of some of the plumb lines, level the plane *without* scales, drop the plumbs, make some chalk lines, and do the measuring separate from the weighing.)

Now it's time to do the math work. A simple four-column table will do it for any airplane. Just add the weights to get the total. Multiply each wheel weight by its moment arm (distance from datum) to get its moment in inch-pounds. Now add up the total moment, then divide this total moment by the total weight to get the CG location (arm), in inches behind datum. That's a lot simpler than the almost-quadratic equation found in some AFMs: CG Arm = (Main Gear Arm) - [(Main Gear Arm - Nose Wheel Arm) x (Nose Weight)/(Total Weight)]

Now we have the Basic Empty Weight since we weighed with full oil plus that two gallons of estimated unusable fuel. And we have the CG arm for this basic empty condition—1,107 pounds at 35.9 inches. That CG arm isn't of much value, but the moment of 39,739 inch-pounds will be needed for all future calculations.

While the airplane is still on the scales, let's find the moment arm for the pilot and passenger seats. *Carefully* load the seats with "average" people, re-check the level, re-check the tailwheel arm (the leaf spring may have flattened a little), and go through the same calculations.

So, we have accurately located the people part of the loading. If the seats are adjustable, it would be best to do this check in a mid-position that most likely fits the average flying position. The same check can be made for the moment arm of the fuel load if the cells are other than box-shaped, and their filled CG can't be accurately determined with a tape measure.

This same check could be made for the rear seats, and that would be a good idea if it's a small plane. A small error in passenger location can be a gross error in a short fuselage. For baggage, it's best to make some tape measurements while the plane is still level. Make a side-view diagram, and note the "arm" measurements of the instrument panel, rear bulkhead, and center of the baggage space.

Now that we have finished the weighing and measuring, let's get this machine off the tail stand before it falls and get it off the scales. Check that the scales still read zero after all of this abuse.

If the airplane really was a homebuilt, or an old classic or an antique without a good loading chart, let's finish up by putting all of these good weight and measure figures into a usable loading table, similar to the ones you find in more contemporary airplane handbooks.

Whoops! One more item to go. Run to the Xerox machine and make a few copies of the new loading table, then spend another hour with a calculator and figure out some extreme loadings. Try one small pilot and no fuel—in a lot of planes that puts you ahead of the forward CG limit line. Or two heavy people and full fuel—is there any weight or CG margin left for baggage?

For those who think they don't need to do this math work because the machine is factory-built, don't kid yourself; lots of the four, six, eight and ten-seaters can't fill all the seats and all of the fuel tanks without being way out of the weight and/or CG limits. The big machines with two motors usually require a careful splitting of the baggage between front and back cargo holds to keep the CG within the flyable range.

All this talk about weights, arms, moments and such can really make the head swim. But, it's important stuff. That bird won't fly well if loaded outside its limits—that's why the designer set the limits. It may be completely *unflyable* if the CG is way overboard. Consider the commuter pilot who very carefully added up the weights of all his passengers, and all of their baggage—even figured the moments for each item of the big load. But, he never totalled the moments, never divided this big moment by the total weight, never really knew that he was horribly tail-heavy. *But, he found out the hard way—he and several of the passengers died in the crash, when the plane went out of control right after liftoff!*

The Human Factor in Aircraft Loading

Given a pilot's education in the hazards that exist when an airplane is loaded too heavily or outside the allowable CG range, it's difficult to understand why some aviators insist on walking near the edge of disaster. In most cases, a few pounds over gross, or a fraction of an inch beyond the CG limit won't generate a disaster, but it's illegal—and poor judgment—just the same. And a pilot never knows what other circumstances might arise to turn an otherwise controllable airplane into a monster.

The occasional foray into the unknown territory of poorly loaded flight characteristics isn't limited to the non-professional pilot— over-gross flying in corporate circles exists, and it is easy to imagine why. First, it takes a secure position for the corporate pilot to dare to tell the president that even though the royal yacht has all those seats, they can't be filled—at least, not legally—and still get the required range out of the ship. Second, once he has done a little over-gross flying in a particular airplane (especially if he's lucky or careful enough to remain within CG limits), a pilot may conclude that there's no grave handling problem, or any reason not to treat the plane as normal in most respects—it's just a tad heavier.

However, once the "fill the seats and let's go" syndrome becomes a habit, it can easily be compounded by other fatal errors, such as loading beyond CG limits. An accident which may have all these elements, and the even more egregious error of attempting a takeoff with ice on the wings and tail, occurred at Paine Field, in Everett, Washington.

It was a Rockwell 700, a rare airplane of which only 32 were built. The big twin commenced a takeoff from Runway 16, got airborne and rose to an estimated 100 feet, then began to settle nose-high, holding this attitude in a shallow left turn before slamming into trees a half-mile off the end of the runway. The pilot and four of his six passengers were killed. Testimony from witnesses and a computation of the airplane loading easily established the causes of the crash.

NTSB investigators calculated the airplane load using known items as well as the passenger weights as reflected on their driver's licenses. The twin was approximately 1,000 pounds over gross at takeoff (7,948 versus a maximum takeoff weight of 6,947), with a CG location 1.6 inches aft of the rear limit.

It is worthwhile to consider how manufacturers arrive at the loading figures they put in their handbooks. For gross weight, they may fly a plane several hundred pounds over what will become the book limit, exploring until some performance parameter (e.g., rate of climb) is just sufficiently above certification requirements. In contrast, the tests for center of gravity position will start with the CG well within bounds and usually slide it aft in small increments until a suitable range is established, or until the test pilot encounters the first hint of uncontrollable or unstable tendencies. The book limit is then set safely forward of this position.

The lesson is simple: A pilot contemplating an over-gross flight may be fairly confident that only performance will suffer, and in any event, that someone before him has tried it and succeeded. But a pilot loading a plane with a drastically aft CG can be certain that he is about to explore a regime where even test pilots fear to tread.

The Rockwell 700 is not a good airplane to use as a test bed for weight and balance experiments. The one involved in the crash had an empty weight of 5,398 pounds, giving it a useful takeoff load of 1,549 pounds. This may seem reasonable, until one considers that it had tankage of 208 gallons, or 1,248 pounds of fuel. Allowing 40 pounds for taxi burnoff, this would give it only a maximum of two people and no baggage to stay legal in a full-fuel takeoff.

Moreover, all the passenger seats as well as the fuel tanks are situated behind the aft CG limit. This means that once the pilot and copilot seats and forward baggage compartments are filled, every ounce of fuel, people or baggage added will tend to drive the CG further and further aft.

In a flight manual superior to many in the industry, Rockwell did call attention to the loading problems, with notes such as: "Aft CG loading is critical when lavatory seat is occupied. A detailed study of passenger and baggage loading should be made." However, we note that in this airplane, even if the pilot had off-loaded the lavatory-seat passenger as well as enough fuel to be exactly at maximum takeoff weight, the mere act of the person in the right seat going to the lavatory on climbout would have put the CG aft of limits! In short, any loading of a Rockwell 700 demands careful calculation.

But this pilot compounded his problems many times over when he failed to have the aircraft deiced. Linemen who helped give the plane an auxiliary power start said they observed the pilot brush loose snow off the wings with a broom, but there was a layer of ice underneath. One of them also told the NTSB investigators, "As he boarded the aircraft I asked him if he wanted to deice the aircraft. He asked me, 'How much?' I told him it was about $5 a gallon. He said to forget it."

The linemen said the plane taxied out with pieces of ice stuck to the wing boots, and patches of snow and ice up to 1-1/2 inches thick covering parts of the wing, fuselage and tail surfaces. It's well known that only a very small amount of surface roughness can virtually destroy a wing's lift.

An ameliorating factor that must be confronted is horsepower. The Rockwell 700's engines are TIO-540 Lycomings, normally rated at 350 hp, but derated to 340 hp in this instance because of external noise limits on takeoff. However, if a pilot chose to ignore the handbook limits, nothing would prevent him from extracting the full 350 hp from the engines. Unfortunately, the "extra" power would be illusory; the pilot may think the plane performs slightly better, but the actual effect would be almost too small to measure (i.e., perhaps 80 feet a minute increased rate of climb).

It is therefore reasonable to conclude that this pilot had enough runway (9,000 feet) to accelerate to liftoff speed, but once out of ground effect, was already in a mush-stall predicament due to the ice on the wings. And to frost the cake, he may well have been totally unable to lower the nose due to the CG position.

Was this an unskilled or untrained pilot? Not at all, judging from the NTSB record. A former Marine airman, he held 2,567 total hours, including 1,834 in helicopters. His commercial license was enhanced by instrument ratings both in airplanes and in helicopters. The 32-year-old pilot had been sent to ground school when his company bought the Rockwell 700, and received 19 hours of dual instruction in it. He had flown it an additional 47 hours as PIC before the accident.

Unfortunately, he apparently had gotten into the habit of flying it heavily loaded. The lineman who regularly serviced the plane told *Aviation Safety* the pilot routinely asked for the tanks to be topped with fuel, and commonly loaded people to fill all the seats.

The lineman also related what unfortunately is a classic story. He said he once overheard the pilot mention to the company president that, in view of the short runway at the destination airport that day, some passengers might have to be left behind. The president replied to this effect: "We paid for all those seats—we ought to be able to fill them."

Two human factors at work here, both of them negative; the president in effect making an operational decision in an area he knew nothing about, and the pilot acceding to his employer's demands with no regard for regulations or safety. A good corporate pilot is not paid for flying the company airplane into or out of tight situations—he's paid to make a safety-related decision and tell the boss "This is not safe...we are not going to fly today."

Handling and Flight Characteristics

If it were possible to do it legally and safely, student pilots would clearly benefit from a demonstration of stability and handling qualities of an airplane loaded beyond its CG limits and maximum allowable weight. Those who have been there—either inadvertently or by design, in a flight-test program—will readily agree that it gets pretty spooky out there beyond the envelope.

Airplanes simply don't behave as advertised when they are improperly loaded. Once again, here's test pilot Bill Kelly with a discussion of some real-world problems with improper loading.

Several years ago I was scheduled to assist in the flight evaluation of a Piper Seneca III. I found myself waiting on the ramp of the local airport for the arrival of the test airplane from a nearby dealer. It finally taxied in, tailskid almost touching the ground, and six *big* guys deplaned and took their baggage out of the aft compartment. As all the weight was unloaded, the tailskid rose, and the fully extended nose strut slowly compressed. Nobody opened the nose baggage door, and when I checked, that compartment was empty.

This plane was a loaded demonstrator, including an oxygen bottle and Janitrol heater behind the rear bulkhead, plus almost all of the avionics gear available on the options list. A later check of Section 6 of the aircraft flight manual verified what had been apparent from the taxi attitude—the plane had been loaded behind the aft CG limit. This pilot got away with it, and a lot of other pilots have done the same. But the Seneca, along with most of its smaller sisters in the Cherokee line, seems to have some margin of acceptable stability and control beyond the prescribed loading limits.

Maybe Piper was just being conservative in setting the rearward limit—or maybe there is a particular regime of flight, outside of normal operations, where the handling qualities *don't* meet the requirements and the plane might get downright squirrelly. I saw this several years ago in a different airplane I was flying for FAA certification tests. Everything was fine until I got to Takeoff Climb, Balked Landing Climb, and Power-On Stall tests. With flaps extended, and high power, the airplane lost most of its longitudinal static stability. At the desired aft CG limit the airplane wanted to "nose up" all by itself if slowed anything below trim speed—and it would nose up all the way to stall. The "fix" involved elevator control system changes *plus* a more conservative aft CG limit.

A manufacturer doesn't set those weight and CG limits arbitrarily. He would like as large an envelope as possible to fully utilize all the seats and baggage space. Much designer math work goes into possible loadings even before the first metal is cut for a prototype. Many hours of aerodynamic calculations are spent figuring tail areas and control system requirements. The guys concerned with airframes often have hassles with the avionics types who want their radar to have priority in the nose of a two-engine bird—and maybe with the other group that wants the nosewheel to retract right into what will have to be a nose baggage compartment.

Why give that any priority to the nose baggage compartment? Because it's really for *removable ballast*—ballast usually in the form of baggage to balance out that big load of people in the rear end. Just because your bird has six, or eight, or 11 seats doesn't mean that you can load them all, and then throw the briefcases in the rear baggage area. Just about any general aviation airplane can be overloaded weight-wise if you fill all of the seats and all of the fuel cells. But most of them can be kept within the CG limits if the load is distributed properly.

Your plane doesn't have to be a big one to get into the "overweight" and/or "outside CG limits" category. Even a Cherokee or a Cessna 152 has its loading problems. If you don't like to calculate weight and balance, maybe you need to try flying an old side-by-side machine like the Taylorcraft, Luscombe, or Ercoupe. The Taylorcraft "A" model, with 40 horsepower, didn't even have elevator trim—you just couldn't load it with enough to get it past the aerodynamic limits or to where trim was really a requirement. Of course, these birds usually only gave you a little hanging canvas sack for baggage, with just enough room for a lunch pail and a change of skivvies.

How bad can a misloading be? Pretty bad. Let me quote a portion of the NTSB report on what has to be about the worst example of overweight and aft CG: "...nose-high attitude shortly after takeoff...began to roll to left...then right wing down attitude...then pitched up...left wing down...right wing down...losing altitude...struck the ground...1,060 pounds over allowable takeoff weight...about 8 inches beyond max allowable rear limit...line crew had to wait for the aircraft to move before they could remove the tail stand...witness saw the nosewheel leave the ground occasionally while the aircraft was being taxied out...takeoff roll and rotation were normal...pitched up steeply to 30- to 35-degree attitude... pushed the yoke forward as hard as he could...could not bring the nose down...like a leaf coming from a tree." The accident left eight people dead, 13 wounded!

To be sure, this wasn't your average GA twin—it was a small four-motor commuter, DH-114 Heron, with 21 people on board. The results could be just as catastrophic in today's light or medium twin or single. This plane was badly misloaded—way too heavy— but it still flew...for a short while. Then the extreme aft CG took the airplane beyond the limits of stability—it was *out of control*—no down-elevator left, and it was still nosing up!

Yes, I've flown planes overgross too. And I'd guess that a lot of our readers would admit to the same. There also may be a bunch of "Gee, I don't know—I didn't calculate the weight and CG, but it sure was heavy" types. The people who ferry small planes overseas typically get a Special Airworthiness ticket for up to 25 percent over gross—but with *no relaxing of CG limits*. And along with this "Special" ticket comes an "operating limits" statement, "No flight over populated areas." Interpretation: "You may kill yourself, but don't endanger innocent bystanders."

Most any airplane with wheels at the bottom of the gear struts will *eventually* lift off, no matter what its weight—reference the *Voyager* and the *Spirit of St. Louis*. But climb performance and ceiling will be way down. And stall speed may occur just about at the speed you try for climb. (If you are in a seaplane, you may be a little safer—a machine with floats below the struts, or a boat hull, sometimes signals its unwillingness to fly by refusing to accelerate to liftoff speed when overloaded.)

The NTSB and the FAA don't have the time or the facilities to get concerned with those who fly beyond the weight and CG limits—*until you have a crunch*. Then they get mad. But crunch a bird in an overloaded/misloaded condition, and one guy walks away smiling—*your insurance agent!* You just let him off the hook. You violated the limits of the policy, and he probably won't have to pay a cent on the hull or liability coverages. Your best friend in the right seat, and his family in the back suddenly become kilo-buck or mega-buck liabilities to *you*, the pilot who exceeded the limitations. Even if you don't live through the crash, your estate will likely be eaten alive by the legal process trying to defend your stupidity against all claimants.

Probably the most dangerous misloading is the beyond-aft-CG one—Ol' Lardass. Some pilots will tell you that they like to fly this way: "It's more efficient; I get rid of the down load on the horizontal tail." You gain maybe a hair more efficiency, but that negative lift on the tailfeathers is also the vector that provides positive pitch stability. And if you get to the extremes of the DH-114 I mentioned earlier, that horizontal surface, even with full-down elevator, can't provide enough *up-vector* to counter a pitch-up.

But even before running out of control in a tail-heavy condition comes loss of stability. I've heard pilots say, "Any good pilot can handle that." Sure, up to a point, in the right conditions—daylight, good horizon, no big airspeed divergence—maybe a pilot can handle some pitch instability. But visualize what happens as the CG moves aft. First the "stick-fixed static longitudinal stability" goes to zero, then goes negative. All this big term means is that, when unstable, if you are trimmed at, say, 120 knots, with the elevator at, say zero degrees, you will need *more down elevator* to stabilize at any lower airspeed—or additional *up elevator* for higher speeds.

Studies have shown that pilots don't really fly by cockpit control position, but rather by control force changes. Okay, then depending on the elevator control rig, let the CG get a little further aft of the "stick-fixed" instability point just discussed, and you are into unstable "stick-free static longitudinal stability," meaning the control wheel or stick forces are reversed. It still takes back-wheel to get the nose started up, but once stabilized it then takes a *push* force to hold a speed slower than trim or a pull force to keep the nose from dropping farther if you get above trim speed. Gimmicks such as downsprings and bobweights can give reasonable force stability aft of the CG when elevator position stability goes to pot, but only a *little* farther aft.

Also, as the CG moves aft, the airplane gets more "twitchy"— pitch attitude changes rapidly and with very little control force. Just a little farther back with that CG and "maneuvering stability" becomes another instability—roll into a bank and start a turn, and it may take *push* force to keep the turn from tightening itself! Now even "any good pilot" has a problem, and the airplane may react quicker than the pilot.

All of this can happen even *before* running out of control. There may still be adequate control surface deflection available, but the human isn't quick enough to apply it in the correct direction. That strange Grumman X-29, with the forward-swept wings, flies in this unstable regime all the time—but it's "fly-by-wire" and with quadruple-redundant computers to keep the pilot out of trouble, lots of gyros, accelerometers, and angle of attack sensors.

A twin-turboprop crash in 1977 brought on an NTSB-sponsored flight test program. Calspan was commissioned to configure their variable-stability B-26 to fly like the subject turboprop at various CG positions including the alleged extreme-far-aft loading of the accident. Since the B-26 would be "flying-by-wire" during the tests, not really loaded into an unstable regime, evaluations could be conducted in a condition that would have been extremely unsafe in the actual airplane. The B-26 safety pilot could at any time revert to manual control, get rid of the "fly-by-wire-and-computer" instability, and take over from the test pilot. With the accident airplane's loading simulated, the test pilots found the turboprop to be nearly uncontrollable.

Here are some excerpts from the NTSB's report of this misloaded twin's crash: "Control characteristics degraded significantly...CG well aft of certificated limits...pilot's inability to control a longitudinally unstable aircraft during a climbing turn in instrument meteorological conditions...left turn after takeoff...turn of about 270 deg to the right...turn of about 180 deg to the left...series of shallow climbs and descents during the turns...out of the overcast in a steep descent which continued into the ground...at takeoff, the CG 2.09" to 3.2" aft of approved rear limit...flight characteristics which were both statically and dynamically unstable...stick force-airspeed gradients would have been reversed...maneuvering stick force-load factor gradient would have been essentially zero..." (This is getting hairy, isn't it? But wait, there's more!) "Any inattention to aircraft control would quickly precipitate aircraft divergence...the time to double pitch divergence amplitude is about 2 seconds...." (This means that if the nose has come up five degrees above the desired attitude, two seconds later it will be 10 degrees high without correction, or four seconds later will be 20 degrees up!)

Near the end, the narrative gets real descriptive: "He may have merely modulated the divergence of the aircraft for a brief time before matters became uncontrollable by periodically pushing and pulling on the control wheel in an attempt to set pitch attitude...overcontrolled the aircraft into an unsafe condition during recovery attempts...overcontrol then increased in amplitude until the aircraft crashed...."

Sure, those are excerpts, just like the preceding DH-114 account. But they are not taken out of context. Both of these planes got out of control...and I believe that *pilots* are responsible for the vast majority of the "out-of-control" stall-and-spin crashes. Well, here's another variety of mishap that can be blamed on us pilots. *Pilots* are responsible for the proper loading of the airplane. Sure, the dispatch and baggage-handling crews were in hot water for the misloading of the DH-114, and maybe the pilot was misled by the tailstand holding up a fanny end that would have otherwise been drooping during his preflight, but, it's still the PIC's job to ensure a safe loading.

This doesn't mean necessarily working out a complete weight/CG problem for every flight—especially if you have already spent a few hours working out some "extreme" loadings. A handy insert for any AFM is a few sample loadings that approach the maximum weight, forward CG and aft CG limits. Such as: With full fuel, how much cabin weight can be carried? How much baggage? Is the plane beyond a "zero-fuel" weight limit? Is the CG getting close to the line? Is CG still okay after all the fuel has been used?

If weight-wise, your big nine-seater can carry a load of people with sufficient fuel for the trip, but CG is out of bounds to the rear, maybe you need to trot down to the building supply store and pick up a few 40-pound bags of sand or gravel for the nose baggage compartment. Don't blame the manufacturer if your bird is hard to load; he gave you just what you asked for—lots of seats, baggage space, and large fuel tanks. He gave you flexibility in loading and range. You have to be flexible in how you use the available space.

Marketing brochures often state on one line, "Range—1000 miles." The next line then states, "six-place." Down near the bottom you find, "Baggage area volume—40 cubic feet." Yeah, but these sales claims are no substitute for the weight and balance section of the AFM. There is almost nothing flying that can stay within limits if you fill everything—fuel, seats, baggage compartments. Not even that little two-seat trainer, usually.

Several years ago I observed the landing of a big six-place single—it was more arrival than landing—as it touched down very hard on its nosegear and went through several bad porpoise cycles before coming to a stop with no damage. The plane was lightly loaded—partial fuel and only two people with baggage—but this pair, father and son, were in the front seats, and *each* weighed just about 300 pounds. And the baggage (quite a bit of it, and heavy) was in the nose baggage compartment, right behind the firewall. Gross weight was within limits, but CG was way ahead of the forward limit. So, naturally, as airspeed dwindled during landing flare, the stabilator ran out of poop, and even full-back wheel couldn't get the nose up to touchdown attitude. This plane came equipped with one of those nifty Piper "Weight and Balance Visual Plotters"—still sealed in its cellophane envelope, unused.

Yes, nose-heavy loadings can hurt you too. Especially in a taildragger. In addition to the noseover possibilities, landings and takeoffs can be hairy. On takeoff the tail might come up so fast and so far that the prop strikes the runway. The forward CG at light weight is frequently set by test results as the point beyond which you can't make a three-point landing at idle. For taildragger pilots, imagine the feeling during the flare when you reach full-back-wheel and the nose *starts to drop!*

As noted earlier, some guys consider themselves such "good airplane drivers" that they can handle a stability problem. But how about structural failure? Here are some excerpts—again from FAA's special issue Airworthiness Alerts of 6/18/87 on the V-Tail Bonanza: The FAA said the plane's "...ease of...outside the aft center of gravity limits" could mean that an "...inexperienced or inattentive pilot could exceed the allowable flight envelope." More excerpts: "...maneuvering stability...was light at the most aft CG and becomes lighter beyond the aft limit...structural design limit of the airplane can easily be exceeded with little pilot effort...low elevator control forces can be masked by elevator control friction...airframe failure caused by structural overload becomes a possibility when the airplane is flying beyond the aft CG limits...."

That last paragraph really applies to any airplane, not just V-Tails. Beech is catching the flak because it's easy to misload this model. A real easy way to misload is to be working with an erroneous empty or basic weight, CG, or moment.

The Bottom Line of Aircraft Loading

Whoever said that "aviation, like the sea, is not inherently dangerous, but it is terribly unforgiving of any carelessness, incapacity or neglect" may have had aircraft loading in mind when that memorable statement was made. Almost without exception, an airplane will perform as advertised as long as the operator respects its limitations, especially when it comes to weight and balance. But when an aircraft is loaded beyond its certificated limits of weight and CG location, the pilot is sometimes merely along for the ride. Loss of control is definitely not a happy event in one's aeronautical experience.

There's a long history of loading-related accidents in the aerial trucking business, in which some pilots knuckle under to the theory that says "if we can load everything and get the doors closed, it'll fly." Making money is the name of the game under Part 135 or 121, but unfortunately airplanes don't know what part of the FARs apply to a flight—airplanes respond only to the immutable laws of physics and aerodynamics.

We close this section with two accident reports, both of which are classics in their own way; they demonstrate complete disregard for physical laws and aviation regulations, and a wealth of misplaced optimism about what an airplane can do.

An ATP and his companion, also an Airline Transport Pilot, were killed when their Twin Beech rolled over and dove into the ground shortly after liftoff at Miami International Airport on a cargo flight bound for Fort Myers, Florida.

The PIC's personal records indicated more than 10,000 total hours as a pilot; his partner was not officially part of the crew, but apparently was along for the experience.

The plane was observed by witnesses to roll about 1,000 feet before the tailwheel came off the ground, although one witness stated the tailwheel never did come off. After a total ground roll of about 3,000 feet (that's a lot for a Twin Beech!), the plane became airborne, pitched up to a near-vertical attitude, then rolled over and dove back to the ground from 100 feet AGL.

The NTSB investigator, who used conservative estimates of fuel, cargo and occupant weights, figured the plane was at least 800 pounds over its maximum allowable takeoff weight and the CG was well beyond the aft center of gravity limit. Among the items aboard were 2,240 pounds worth of tractor parts, steel dollies, and two steel cylinders on a pallet just inside the cabin door.

The investigator also noted that the right-seat pilot's weight had been listed as 160 pounds on the loading document, but someone had drawn a line through the item and had not included it in the total weight. Also missing from the manifest, 50 gallons of fuel in the rear tanks.

The second accident occurred in a more organized setting—a scheduled commuter flight from Pittsburgh to Johnstown, Pennsylvania, with a very experienced captain in command. The aircraft was a Beech 99A.

The ceiling varied from 200 to 400 feet that night at Johnstown, and visibility was 2 miles in very light snow and fog. The flight was cleared for a localizer approach, but struck the approach lighting system and an embankment, coming to rest about 200 feet short of the runway. Fifteen passengers and two crewmembers were aboard, but only the first officer and four passengers survived.

That's a full load for a Beech 99, and although the NTSB concluded that the accident was caused by a premature descent below a safe approach slope followed by a stall and loss of aircraft control, the weight and CG location played a part.

Air carriers are permitted to use standard passenger weights (this procedure requires approval by the FAA, of course) and in this case the computed weight at takeoff from Pittsburgh would have been 10,797 pounds, or 397 pounds more than permitted for the airplane. There was a lot of last-minute activity before the flight taxied from the gate, and the first officer filled out a load manifest on the way to Johnstown; this document indicated a gross takeoff weight of 10,391 pounds, arrived at by ignoring 400 pounds of fuel that was known to be in the tanks. (It later was discovered that "keeping two set of books" was standard operating procedure for this airline.)

When actual numbers were applied to the loading calculations during the investigation, the aircraft weight at impact was determined to be approximately 10,100 pounds—well below the maximum landing weight—but the CG was located 1.12 inches beyond the aft limit.

The captain was known to fly slower-than-normal approaches in low-visibility conditions, and with the CG out of limits aft, aircraft response to control and power inputs were probably less than optimum. The first officer said that just before impact he felt a definite increase in the sink rate—perhaps because of downdrafts known to exist at the approach end of this runway—and even though the captain applied full power, the airplane continued to descend until it hit the lights.

The NTSB report included a telling paragraph with regard to the company's loading practices: "The first officer and other former pilots testified that it was a regular company practice to enter low fuel weights on the load manifests when 15 passengers were aboard. The low fuel weights were entered to show that the aircraft was within weight and balance limits. They also stated that passenger seats were never restricted from use to keep the aircraft within weight and balance limits. It was an unwritten company policy to accept additional passengers and to fly the aircraft overweight and out of CG limits if necessary."

Takeoff and Climb Performance

A critical observer at a busy general aviation airport would probably mark down a number of Cs, perhaps some Ds, and maybe even an F or two if the objective were to grade the takeoff techniques of pilots. Some of them keep the nosewheel on the ground until a certain airspeed is attained, then rotate; some lighten the load on the nose gear early in the takeoff roll and hold that attitude until the airplane lifts off, and others have no takeoff technique. It's a matter of whatever works to make the airplane fly.

And we have to ask, so what? If the airplane gets off the ground safely and doesn't use up all the runway, does takeoff technique really matter? We'd be terribly naive and would miss the mark of educational responsibility if we agreed. Takeoff technique *is* important—perhaps not on every departure—but just about every pilot will sooner or later come up against a situation in which he must squeeze all the performance out of his airplane, and if his technique has been "whatever works," the outcome may be something less than desirable.

At the outset of this volume of *Command Decisions*, we suggested that x amount of thrust should propel y amount of weight down the runway and cause it to become airborne in z number of feet. Of course, the validity and reliability of that premise depends on the atmospheric conditions at the time, the weight of the airplane, the condition of the runway, and it depends very heavily on the way the pilot handles the controls.

"X number of feet" can be calculated using the takeoff performance charts in the Pilot's Operating Handbook for any airplane, as well as the proper technique to make it happen. The manufacturer doesn't tell you how much pressure to apply to the controls, or how rapidly to change the pitch attitude; but you are provided with a recommended procedure and the desired results, usually in terms of airspeed at certain points in the takeoff.

Our objective in this section is to refresh your knowledge of normal takeoff performance and offer some suggestions for improving your technique—as well as to provide some illustrations of how *not* to do it.

Just How Good Can You Get?

Much has been made of the accuracy of aircraft performance charts. Is it realistic to expect your Cessna 172 to be 50 feet in the air in exactly 1440 feet from brake release on a standard day at sea level? That's what the handbook says, but that's also with a certification test pilot at the controls of a brand-new airplane and optimum conditions all around. Of course that's an unrealistic expectation, but it provides a solid foundation for planning a takeoff. The pilot who starts down a 1440-foot runway with a stand of 50-foot pine trees at the end is kidding himself, and asking for trouble. Treat these numbers tenderly; they should be considered guidelines, and you might safely add 100 percent to the book figures to cover inexperience or infrequent flying or getting acquainted with a new (to you) make or model. That percentage can be reduced as you get better at your business, but operating with no fudge factor at all—i.e. depending on book performance figures to match operational requirements—is not a safe procedure.

The certification rules allow no procedure or technique that requires test-pilot skill, and the people who develop the performance charts take that into account. The figures that get published in the POH are probably a pretty good middle ground between the pilot techniques of a Chuck Yeager and a ham-handed beginner. We repeat: Treat these numbers as guidelines, and back off when there is any doubt of completing a flight operation safely.

A Look at the Charts

Manufacturers present the results of their performance tests in one of two ways—tables, or graphs. Why don't they get together and decide on one way to do it? Same reason they don't get together

Figure 3-1

TAKEOFF DISTANCE
MAXIMUM WEIGHT 3800 LBS

SHORT FIELD

CONDITIONS:
Flaps 10°
2700 RPM and 36.5 Inches Hg Prior to Brake Release
Mixture Set at 186 PPH
Cowl Flaps Open
Paved, Level, Dry Runway
Zero Wind

NOTES:
1. Short field technique as specified in Section 4.
2. Landing gear extended until takeoff obstacle is cleared.
3. Decrease distances 10% for each 10 knots headwind. For operation with tailwinds up to 10 knots, increase distances by 10% for each 2.5 knots.
4. For operation on a dry, grass runway, increase distances by 15% of the "ground roll" figure.

WEIGHT LBS	TAKEOFF SPEED KIAS		PRESS ALT FT	0°C		10°C		20°C		30°C		40°C	
	LIFT OFF	AT 50 FT		GRND ROLL	TOTAL TO CLEAR 50 FT OBS	GRND ROLL	TOTAL TO CLEAR 50 FT OBS	GRND ROLL	TOTAL TO CLEAR 50 FT OBS	GRND ROLL	TOTAL TO CLEAR 50 FT OBS	GRND ROLL	TOTAL TO CLEAR 50 FT OBS
3800	68	75	S.L.	1010	1665	1100	1815	1200	1990	1310	2180	1430	2400
			1000	1075	1760	1170	1925	1280	2110	1395	2315	1525	2555
			2000	1145	1865	1250	2040	1360	2235	1485	2460	1625	2715
			3000	1215	1975	1330	2165	1450	2375	1585	2615	1735	2895
			4000	1295	2095	1415	2295	1550	2525	1695	2785	1855	3090
			5000	1385	2225	1510	2440	1650	2690	1810	2970	1980	3295
			6000	1475	2365	1615	2595	1765	2865	1930	3170	2115	3525
			7000	1575	2515	1725	2765	1885	3055	2065	3285	2265	3775
			8000	1685	2675	1845	2950	2020	3260	2210	3620	2425	4050

and decide on either electrical or hydraulic landing gear systems, plain or Fowler flaps, plungers or levers for power controls. It's a free country; some airplane builders prefer tables, some prefer graphic presentations.

Figure 3-1 is a typical tabular performance chart. We'll come back to the operational conditions and procedures later on, but for now, notice the columns that contain values for airplane weight, pressure altitude and air temperature; these are the three most important factors in determining takeoff performance (or any kind of performance, for that matter) for any aircraft. To use the chart, simply find the correct pressure altitude line, move across to the appropriate temperature column, and read the takeoff distances.

Figure 3-2 is another "chart of tables" this one differing only in format; altitudes and temperatures have changed places, but the outcome is the same.

Figure 3-3 is a typical performance chart in a graphic format. The slope of the lines represents the effect of each of the conditions we just mentioned. Notice, for example that any reduction in airplane weight at a given altitude-temperature combination will result in a shorter takeoff distance. To use this chart, insert the numbers that apply to your takeoff condition and follow the profile of the dashed-line example.

No matter who built the airplane (even if you built it yourself!) takeoff performance will be presented in one of these formats, or slight variations thereof. That makes it easy—learn one, you've learned 'em all!

(Just for illustration, we've included a more complicated chart for a more complicated airplane [Figure 3-4] to show that other performance conditions can be added; in this case the effects of runway gradient [slope], the use of pneumatic anti-ice systems [thrust thieves], and the availability of clearway—a "runway extension" applicable only to turbine-powered airplanes in engine-failure circumstances.)

Aircraft weight is usually presented in convenient increments to ease the pain of performance calculations. Notice that Piper provides a near-infinite range of weights (Figure 3-3), while the Cessna Skylane handbook contains this chart (Figure 3-1) for maximum allowable takeoff weight and other similar charts for lower weights. The Beech Sierra information represents performance to be expected at maximum weight, and there's a note that

Figure 3-2

NORMAL TAKE-OFF DISTANCES

ASSOCIATED CONDITIONS

POWER	2700 RPM, FULL THROTTLE
FLAPS	UP
GEAR	RETRACT AFTER LIFT-OFF
RUNWAY	PAVED, LEVEL, DRY SURFACE
WEIGHT	2750 LBS
TAKE-OFF SPEEDS	LIFT-OFF 80 MPH/70 KTS/IAS
	50 FT 84 MPH/73 KTS/IAS

NOTE

FOR EACH 100 POUNDS BELOW 2750 LBS, REDUCE TABULATED DISTANCES BY 8% AND TAKE-OFF SPEEDS BY 1 MPH

WIND COMPONENT DOWN RUNWAY KNOTS	SEA LEVEL			2000 FEET			4000 FEET			6000 FEET			8000 FEET		
	OAT °F	GROUND ROLL FEET	TOTAL OVER 50 FT OBSTACLE FEET	OAT °F	GROUND ROLL FEET	TOTAL OVER 50 FT OBSTACLE FEET	OAT °F	GROUND ROLL FEET	TOTAL OVER 50 FT OBSTACLE FEET	OAT °F	GROUND ROLL FEET	TOTAL OVER 50 FT OBSTACLE FEET	OAT °F	GROUND ROLL FEET	TOTAL OVER 50 FT OBSTACLE FEET
0	23	1079	1714	16	1265	1997	9	1486	2332	2	1748	2728	-6	2061	3198
	41	1158	1845	34	1370	2151	27	1611	2516	20	1898	2946	13	2341	3458
	59	1260	1980	52	1480	2312	45	1742	2706	38	2054	3173	31	2429	3728
	77	1356	2120	70	1594	2478	63	1879	2904	56	2218	3408	49	2624	4009
	95	1456	2265	88	1713	2650	81	2021	3108	74	2388	3651	67	2829	4300
15	23	942	1496	16	1108	1749	9	1305	2048	2	1540	2403	-6	1821	2824
	41	1021	1613	34	1201	1886	27	1417	2213	20	1674	2599	13	1983	3059
	59	1103	1734	52	1300	2031	45	1535	2384	38	1814	2803	31	2152	3303
	77	1189	1859	70	1402	2179	63	1657	2561	56	1962	3014	49	2328	3556
	95	1278	1988	88	1508	2333	81	1785	2744	74	2115	3233	67	2512	3818
30	23	805	1278	16	950	1500	9	1124	1764	2	1332	2078	-6	1580	2452
	41	874	1381	34	1032	1621	27	1223	1910	20	1450	2251	13	1724	2660
	59	946	1487	52	1120	1749	45	1327	2061	38	1574	2432	31	1875	2877
	77	1021	1597	70	1209	1880	63	1435	2218	56	1705	2620	49	2031	3103
	95	1100	1711	88	1303	2016	81	1548	2380	74	1841	2815	67	2195	3336

directs pilots to reduce distances by 8 percent for each 100 pounds below the 2750-pound maximum.

Obviously, altitudes and temperatures and weights don't always have values that coincide with the lines and numbers on the charts. The Piper graph requires finding the point between labeled lines for such values, and the tabular charts require interpolation—correcting the published number by the appropriate amount. It will often be necessary to do a double interpolation, and it doesn't matter where you start; correct one value, then apply that to the other. Remember that "close" counts only when you're throwing horseshoes and hand-grenades. These numbers are guidelines. (Have we said that before?)

Time Out for Thin Air

Before we press on, here's a primer on density altitude—the result of correcting pressure altitude for non-standard temperature.

All around the country each summer, this scene is enacted regularly: A fully loaded, low-horsepower airplane gallops blithely down a moderately long runway and deposits itself at the end of it. The pilot clambers out of the wreckage looking for a mechanic to prove that "something was wrong with this airplane." Only after some thought (which should have taken place during preflight) will the pilot recognize the real problem—density altitude.

We conducted a thorough study of "density altitude" accidents, the performance characteristics of common airplanes in high density altitude situations, and the dubious nature of the official explanation of the phenomenon. The results lead to some conclusions that may seem obvious (but didn't to the pilots involved) and some that are downright surprising. For instance, "density altitude" is an FAA term which knowledgeable agency officials tell us is inaccurate and probably should be deleted or modified. However, there is no FAA effort under way to do so, and current FAA publications continue to use "density altitude" as the official term. For reasons that will be explained below, most makers of airplanes do not use the term at all. We will use it in quotation marks throughout this article, to call attention to its questionable nature.

Although the high, hot, humid conditions in question affect all airplanes, the "density altitude" accident has an 84 percent likelihood of happening to a single-engine fixed-wing aircraft—rather

Figure 3-3

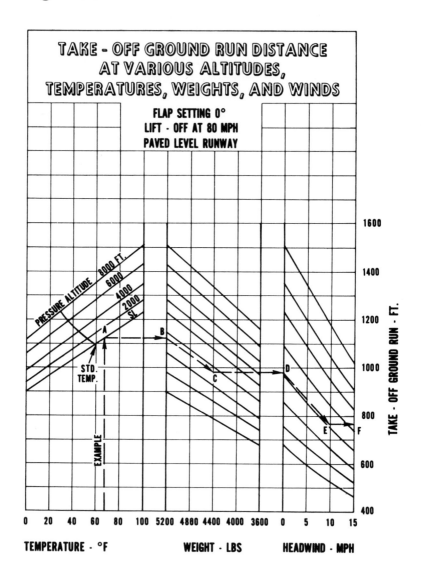

than a twin (6 percent) or a helicopter (10 percent).

Agricultural aircraft account for about 18 percent of "density altitude" accidents, but almost none of the fatalities. Forty-six percent of the time, the accident involves an aircraft with all its seats filled, but only 9 percent are calculated to be over gross.

Popular belief may have it that inexperienced pilots flying from their lowland home bases to mountainous airports are most likely to have "density altitude" accidents. Within our ability to discern it, we believe this is not the case. The pilots involved in such accidents are definitely experienced, both in total hours and in type, and we find a likelihood that they are not itinerant, either.

As might be expected, 66 percent of "density altitude" accidents occur during takeoff, 22 percent in cruise (mainly in high mountain blind canyons), 5 percent in go-arounds and 7 percent in landings (mainly overshoots).

July is the most likely month for "density altitude" accidents, California the most likely state, noon to 6 p.m. the most likely time period, and a Piper Cherokee the most likely airplane. Typical conditions may involve a temperature of 79 degrees F and a computed "density altitude" of 7,100 feet.

What Is It?

The concept of "density altitude" has been popularized by the FAA in an attempt to educate pilots on the drastic decreases in airplane performance which occur on high, hot, humid days. All airplanes suffer in performance as the altitude increases, but many airplanes suffer extra performance losses as the temperature also increases, and as the humidity rises. Unfortunately, the FAA concept is inaccurate when put into practice. It does not account for humidity at all, nor the substantial differences between normally aspirated and turbocharged engines.

For scientific study, the air is assumed to be "standard" and to have a predictable decrease in pressure as altitude increases. The assumption starts at 29.92 inches of mercury at sea level and decreases the pressure approximately one inch of mercury for each 1,000 feet of altitude. The standard atmosphere also assumes a starting temperature of 15 degrees C. (59 F) and a loss of about two degrees per 1,000 feet.

In fact, the standard atmosphere almost never occurs in real

Figure 3-4

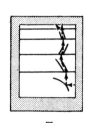

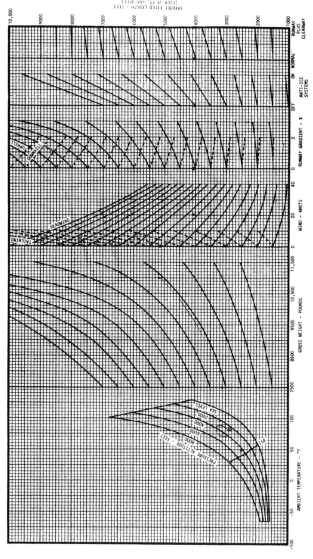

**TAKEOFF FIELD LENGTH
(OVER 35 FOOT OBSTACLE)**

CONDITIONS:

Landing Gear - DOWN   Inoperative Engine - WINDMILLING AFTER V_1
Wing Flaps - T.O. & APPR. Operative Engine - TAKEOFF THRUST
Speed Brakes - RETRACT

life. At a given altitude, it's sometimes hotter than it's "supposed to be," and sometimes cooler. Weather systems vary the atmospheric pressure, which makes a given elevation "higher" or "lower" than standard. The FAA concept of "density altitude" aims to account for these variations.

For instance, a sea-level airport on a standard day will have a barometer reading of 29.92 and a temperature of 15 degrees C. But on a hot summer day, the numbers might be 29.82 and 30 C. According to the "density altitude" concept, the airport can now be considered to have an effective altitude of nearly 2,000 feet—that's the altitude to use for predicting airplane performance.

By inference, a reasonable pilot concludes that it's possible to have two airports with different elevation-temperature combinations that work out to the same "density altitude" and therefore involve the same airplane performance. For convenience, let's assume we're talking about Loveland, Colorado, (elevation 5,015 feet) and Hastings, Nebraska, (elevation 1,954 feet). The pilot at Loveland would have no trouble recognizing that he's in mountainous terrain, while at Hastings, it would seem like a rolling plain.

If it happened that standard pressure prevailed and the temperature at Loveland were 6 C., a pilot using the FAA concept would compute an effective, or "density altitude" of 5,000 feet. If the temperature at Hastings were 38 C, the pilot there would also compute "density altitude" as 5,000 feet. The concept predicts that airplane takeoff, climb and landing performance will be equal in the two situations.

Unfortunately, this is wrong. In a normally aspirated aircraft, the pilot could expect approximately 5 percent better performance on takeoff at Hastings than at Loveland. In a turbocharged aircraft, he could expect about 12 percent better performance at Loveland than at Hastings.

We hasten to add that the general notion of "density altitude" is not faulty, since either airplane will do better at sea level on a standard day than at altitude or on a hot day. But it is wrong to assume that two equal "density altitude" situations are in fact equal in their effect on the airplane.

And there is a further inherent error; the FAA does not account for humidity (nor do the engine and airframe manufacturers) and this can have important consequences.

The air absorbs and holds moisture in relation to its temperature. On a cold day, even if the weatherman reports 100 percent relative humidity, the air may have a negligible amount of water vapor in it. But on a very hot day at 100 percent humidity, the water vapor content is substantial—perhaps 4 to 5 percent of a given pound of air is actually water.

Because the water vapor replaces a portion of oxygen-carrying air entering the engine, it has a "choking" effect on the powerplant. Also, it has a slight cooling effect on combustion. If the mixture is not changed, water vapor alone can cause an engine to run substantially over-rich. In the worst case situation, this could lead to perhaps 8-12 percent less horsepower from the engine, and a magnified decrease in takeoff performance.

Most pilots are not aware of the humidity effect; most airplane manuals do not mention it; most engine operator's manuals ignore it. One FAA publication estimates that if a pilot recognizes a muggy condition on a hot day, he should add 10 percent to the takeoff figure he calculated under the "density altitude" concept.

Cases in Point

High temperature, high altitude takeoffs can require more than lots of runway—sometimes they require more patience and planning instead. The pilot of a Cessna 207 found the combination of density altitude and terrain features to be beyond his aircraft's capabilities during an attempted takeoff from Mackey Bar Airstrip, Idaho. The accident left the aircraft demolished, but the pilot and his passengers on the intended air taxi flight were uninjured.

> This pilot (3,600 hours of flight time) was no stranger to the concept of density altitude and indeed, he took steps to cope with it. He and his four passengers had arrived at the airstrip at 3 p.m., but the pilot decided it was too hot to allow a safe departure from the 2,000-foot MSL field, so he wisely elected to wait until things cooled down.
>
> By 5 p.m., the temperature had dropped to 90 degrees, lowering the density altitude to 4,500 feet. The pilot decided it was time. He boarded his passengers and proceeded to the runway, figured the aircraft could make it out of the 1,900-foot strip with room to spare.

According to the pilot's account of the accident, the takeoff was normal, with the aircraft rotating and lifting off approximately three-quarters of the way down the runway. He reported his airspeed and rate of climb to be "satisfactory" as he passed the end of the runway at about 50 feet AGL.

Off the end of the runway was a river, which cooled the air and apparently produced some downdraft action. As the aircraft crossed the riverbank, it began to sink badly. The pilot tried to exchange some airspeed for altitude, but to no avail.

The aircraft continued to descend as airspeed and altitude ran out. The pilot was able to stretch the flight to the other side of the river, where he crash-landed on the shore. The aircraft was demolished as it bounced across the rough ground, but when it came to a halt the occupants emerged unscathed.

Density altitude bites three times; once in the engine, once in the prop, once in the wings. As the air becomes less dense because of altitude, temperature or humidity (or a combination of all three), the fuel-air mixture must be leaned for best power, which will always be a lower value—that's bite Number One. The prop may spin nearly as fast, but it's displacing fewer molecules of air and thrust suffers—that's bite Number Two. The wings are also experiencing the passage of thinner air, and that means less lift is produced—bite Number Three.

Combine a low-powered airplane with a heavy load and a hot day, and the result will always be miserable takeoff performance. There's simply not enough power or thrust or lift to do the job. Nothing against the Piper Tri-Pacer, but at best it's no skyrocket; with three adults aboard, this one was probably headed for trouble from the start. The pilot's inexperience—a total of 60 hours—didn't help things any.

The takeoff was attempted at 5:10 p.m. on a summer day when the temperature registered 98 degrees. Witnesses saw the Tri-Pacer lift off, but it continued in a nose-high attitude without climbing—classic symptoms of high density altitude, ground effect performance. It passed beneath some high-voltage powerlines as it crossed a highway adjacent to the airport, but the right main landing gear snagged a telephone cable. The plane struck the highway, bounced into the air and touched down again about 80 feet later in a near-vertical position.

Rescuers from vehicles on the highway rushed to remove the occupants, but within a short time a fire started, burning the fabric off the airframe and wings and then spread to the spilled fuel around the aircraft.

The rear-seat passenger was removed and rescuers rolled him over on the ground to extinguish his burning clothing, but both front-seat occupants died in the fire.

Every Camel Has Its Straw

While some accidents occur without warning, there are usually one or more signs of trouble that give a pilot plenty of time to avert disaster. The trick is to recognize the warning flags and act appropriately—unfortunately, it's a judgment call that not all aviators make successfully.

A huge difference between airport elevation and density altitude is not always required to present performance problems that an airplane can't overcome. The situations we've reviewed so far involved very hot days and medium-altitude airports, combining to provide density altitudes that would get any pilot's attention.

In the next illustration, density altitude was only a few feet higher than airport elevation, but the airport was a mile high to start with! Thin air was not the only negative factor at work here; a combination of poor judgment, overloading, failure to check performance data and a possible mechanical failure all conspired with the mile-high elevation to cause the crash of a Piper Lance at Coronado Airport in Albuquerque, New Mexico. The occupants were lucky; two seriously injured, three with minor injuries, and one uninjured.

The takeoff attempt was made on runway 17 at Coronado, a 4,020-foot asphalt strip with a 200-foot overrun area at the departure end. There are 20-foot tall trees located just beyond the end of the runway. The airport is at an elevation of 5,280 feet. The temperature at the time of the accident was approximately 60 degrees F, and with the existing altimeter setting investigators calculated the density altitude to be just over 6,000 feet.

The pilot and one of the passengers had flown from Fort Worth, Texas, to Albuquerque to attend a conference. There were four seats available for the return trip, so the pilot invited his sister, brother-in-law and their two children to fly back to Texas with him.

It was about midday when the pilot preflighted the airplane and confirmed that the tanks had been filled to their 94-gallon maximum capacity. He then loaded the baggage and all five passengers on board, putting the adults in the aft row of seats and the children in the center row. The cabin was warm, so after engine start the pilot turned on the Lance's air conditioner to keep the passengers comfortable.

The Piper air conditioner gets its air supply through a rather large door in the belly of the airplane. The door is electrically operated, extending automatically when the air conditioner is switched on, and retracting when the unit is switched off. Normal operating procedure requires the air conditioner to be off during takeoff; the door causes a lot of drag, and a considerable amount of engine power is required to drive the compressor. The combination results in a significant derogation of takeoff performance. To accommodate the pilot who forgets to follow the procedure, a microswitch relay in the throttle linkage automatically shuts down the air conditioner and retracts the door when full power is applied. The throttle microswitch and the manual on/off switch are not redundant because they use the same electromechanical connections to actuate the condenser door. A failure that prevented the condenser door from closing would probably be in the electromechanical connections, since the likelihood of both switches failing simultaneously is remote.

At the end of the runway, the pilot shut off the air conditioner and commenced the takeoff, but the acceleration didn't feel right, and he chose to abort. He taxied back

A heavy single like Piper's Lance lends itself to overloading and performance-related accidents because pilots assume its six seats can be filled under any and all circumstances.

to the end of the runway to try the takeoff again. While taxiing, he turned the air conditioner on, and took the opportunity to have his passengers change seats—the airplane also felt tail-heavy. The family moved so that the two adults were in the center row of seats and the children were in the back.

The air conditioner was again shut off, and a second takeoff attempt was made. This time, the pilot kept the nose down longer and managed to get the airplane off the ground, but the engine started losing power, so he closed the throttle and aborted the takeoff again.

The airplane was too far down the runway when the takeoff was aborted, and there was insufficient room to stop. The Lance swerved to the right and went off the runway just short of the overrun area, continued for another 230 feet and across a dirt road. It hit a small embankment, collapsing the nosegear and right main landing gear before entering a small cemetery located next

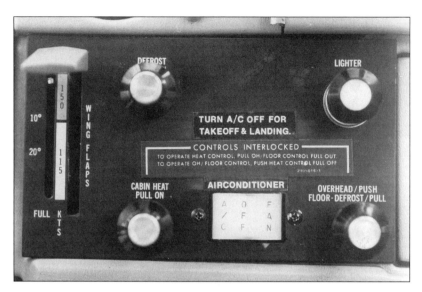

Most air conditioning systems have drag-inducing doors or they rob vital engine horsepower needed for takeoff. For that reason, they should be turned off prior to launch and landing.

to the airport. The Piper struck a tree and a six-foot-high wall next to a statue in the cemetery, and came to rest.

According to witnesses, the first takeoff run was slow; "He was going slow enough that I could run out and catch it," said a lineman for the local FBO. The airplane rotated about halfway down the runway to what one witness described as "an excessive rotation angle." Other witnesses said he rotated sharply two or three times before aborting the first takeoff attempt. The president of the FBO said that the pilot got the main gear off the runway on the third rotation, though another witness said specifically that he did not.

One witness at the FBO thought the pilot would come back to the ramp and shut down, but when he taxied back for another takeoff, the witness considered this unusual enough that he left his office and went out on the ramp to watch. During the second attempt, witnesses said the pilot kept the nosewheel on the ground longer, and again rotated sharply to an excessive angle of attack. They said that the airplane left the ground at a point half-way to three-quarters of the way down the runway, and when it did it was "fundamentally in ground effect." After liftoff it seemed to stagger and came back down immediately.

After the airplane struck the tree and stone wall, the right wing burst into flames, and although witnesses arrived at the scene less than a minute later, the right side of the airplane was fully involved in the fire. The flames were estimated at 20 to 30 feet high, and the cockpit was filling with smoke. The first person on the scene saw the four rear-seat passengers standing on the runway, one of the women shouting "Get them out!" A few of the witnesses approached the airplane and found the right front passenger, who threw himself across the seat backs. He was injured, unable to walk, and had to be dragged from the airplane. The pilot was the last to get out.

The right front seat passenger corroborated the pilot's report of a power failure. He said that during the second takeoff attempt the airplane attained an altitude of 15 to 20 feet and "we lost power, I guess. It seemed like it changed sounds. It seemed like we stalled or something."

A number of witnesses disagreed that the engine failed. "The engine, both times, was running, sound—a good sounding engine. It sounded like it was at its operational capacity. No bumps, no observed carburetion smoke, no nothing. It was running as advertised," reported one witness. Another said "He began his takeoff run with what appeared to be full power." A third said the airplane's engine sounded "strong."

After the accident, the bent propeller and a magneto damaged by the heat of the post-crash fire were replaced, and the engine was put through an operational test. It operated normally, and nothing was noted that could account for a loss of power.

The pilot said that although he used full throttle and a high-rpm propeller setting, he did not lean the engine despite the high density altitude. Thus it is likely that the engine was not producing full rated power for takeoff.

There was also a question regarding the air conditioner. The pilot and front seat passenger both said that it was shut off, but witnesses said that the belly door was open during both takeoff attempts. It was found open at the crash site, and the compressor clutch was engaged.

According to the Pilot's Operating Handbook, a malfunction that prevents the air conditioner from shutting off can reduce climb performance by as much as 100 feet per minute. A malfunction that causes the condenser door to remain open will rob the pilot of 50 feet per minute.

The throttle quadrant and the air-conditioner microswitch were destroyed by the fire, so no determination could be made regarding the switch's role in the accident.

It's debatable whether the Lance would have made it off the airport even with the air conditioner off and the condenser door closed. Investigators performed weight and balance calculations taking into account the exact weight of fuel and the weight of the passengers, but ignoring the effect of baggage. Even without this weight accounted for, the airplane was still determined to be nearly 300 pounds over gross weight at the time of takeoff. Further, the center of gravity was found to be *forward* of the allowable CG location during the second takeoff attempt.

Calculations were also made to determine the takeoff distance required, taking into account the zero-flap condition of the airplane but disregarding the effect of the air conditioner condenser door. Given the existing density altitude and wind conditions, investigators concluded that the Lance would have required a minimum of 2,600 feet of ground roll to get off the ground, and a total of 4,700 feet to clear a 50-foot obstacle.

It's interesting to note that the pilot apparently misinterpreted the poor acceleration he sensed during the first takeoff attempt as nothing more than improper weight distribution. Rather than take the aborted takeoff as a warning to double check his airplane, he simply tried to depart again—with disastrous results.

If the airplane had been within weight and balance limits, the mixture properly leaned, flaps extended to the recommended short-field setting (25 degrees) and reasonably good pilot technique, the takeoff might have been a success. With all the problems the pilot brought on himself, the failure of the air conditioner may well have been the straw that broke the camel's back.

Good Takeoff Technique

Making the numbers work, i.e. getting your airplane off the ground and arriving at an altitude of 50 feet in the prescribed distance (or close thereto) is a function of pilot technique—as long as the engine is in reasonably good condition, and all the conventions on the chart are observed.

At the outset, there are three ways to get things started; a running takeoff (in which the pilot moves onto the runway and keeps right on going—no stopping to line up), a hold-the-brakes-until-full-power takeoff (which explains itself), and a release-the-brakes-add-full-power technique, which also needs no further description. A running takeoff will always get you off the ground somewhat sooner, because some of the inertia is already overcome.

But there's considerable controversy over the other two; is anything gained by turning the engine up to full power before releasing the brakes? Probably not, because a propeller doesn't begin to become efficient until it's moving forward at a pretty good clip. This may not hold true for every airplane and every propeller, but some carefully measured takeoff distances for a Cessna Caravan (the *big* single-engine turboprop) showed surprisingly insignificant differences between the two techniques.

However, take notice that most manufacturers will state in the performance section of the POH that when a takeoff roll is started by releasing the brakes and then opening the throttle, *takeoff distance should be figured from the point where the throttle is completely open.*

Now you have introduced a subjective value—how fast should you open the throttle? Our answer is, as fast as seems reasonable and proper; there is no answer in seconds that would work safely for all powerplants. Just remember that with a large airplane and a slow application of power, you could easily be a thousand feet down the runway before all the horses are working.

When handbook performance is your goal, execute a running takeoff if you can; the brake-hold technique is your next best option.

Pitch attitude is the next thing to consider during a normal takeoff. Check the takeoff performance charts we've presented as examples for single-engine airplanes (multi-engine technique and requirements come in a later section); each of them specifies an

Even in a STOL-equipped airplane, squeezing maximum performance out of an airplane at takeoff requires a high level of proficiency.

indicated airspeed for lift-off and another—slightly higher—that you should attain as you reach 50 feet above the ground.

For normal operations, where absolute attainment of handbook figures is not a requirement, but a smooth, positive, passenger-pleasing departure is your goal, here's a technique that satisfies all the requirements. While you sit in the pilot's seat, have someone lower the tail of your airplane until the nosewheel just clears the ground (this is obviously not to be done with the engine running); take notice of this pitch attitude, and pick out a visual cue that you can always rely on—the top of the glare shield will probably appear very close to the horizon, for example.

To apply this "normal takeoff" technique, smoothly and slowly raise the nose to the target attitude just as soon as the elevators become active in the takeoff roll, and hold this attitude until the airplane flies off the ground. It's as simple as that. Be prepared to make some adjustments as airspeed increases; the faster the airplane moves, the more effective the elevators become, and a given amount of control deflection will provide an increasing pitch attitude. If you hold the elevator position required to get the nose to the takeoff attitude, you'll wind up with an attitude much too high, and defeat the purpose of the technique. How much of a change? Whatever it takes to keep the nose on the horizon, or whatever your visual cue happens to be. You can adjust the pitch attitude as required to attain and maintain the appropriate climb airspeed.

Special Techniques for High Density Altitude Takeoffs

Ground effect is at once a blessing and a curse when you're trying to get an airplane off the ground in a high density altitude situation. Oh, you can get it *off* well enough—ground effect is a significant blessing when the wings are very close to the surface—but try to gain altitude by increasing the pitch attitude slightly and the airplane sinks. The curse is that you have to stay very close to the ground to continue flying. Few pilots are able to exercise the discipline required to recognize what's happening and fly it out. With power fixed at maximum, the *only* solution to the problem is to remain in ground effect as long as possible, and hope that the airplane will accelerate to an airspeed that will permit a climb.

Ground effect decreases exponentially with altitude, and for all practical purposes has disappeared at one wing-span's height. If there's enough clear terrain ahead to permit acceleration while the plane is still in ground effect, there's no problem; but that circumstance doesn't prevail around very many airports. Talk about being between rocks and hard places! Can't climb, can't accelerate, can't turn, don't want to land; there's nothing to be done except apply Rule Number One—fly the airplane—and hope for the best.

Most of the takeoff accidents in which density altitude played a role were the result of a pilot trying to force an airplane (usually heavily loaded) into the air prematurely because the runway wasn't long enough. Ground effect aids and abets what appears to be a normal liftoff, but then the airplane balks—it simply won't climb more than a few feet off the deck. The end of the runway is approaching rapidly, perhaps a row of trees or a building, or perhaps the pilot feels a need to climb even though there's plenty of runway remaining—and when he applies a bit of back pressure to the wheel, there's nothing to overcome the additional drag and the airplane sinks to the point where ground effect will support it at the new angle of attack. This sequence may continue, using up valuable energy all the while, until the airspeed gets so low that the wings stall and deposit the airplane on the ground, or until there's an impact with something else.

This problem can be circumvented by first adding a generous fudge factor (certainly not less than 50 percent) to the calculated takeoff distance, and if the result is more feet than there is runway available, download the airplane, wait for more wind or less temperature. Second, with plenty of runway available, plan to keep the airplane on the ground long enough to build up perhaps 10-15 knots beyond the normal rotation speed, then rotate gently and climb only a few feet. Let the airplane fly level in ground effect until the airspeed reaches the target value for climb, then gently increase pitch attitude and climb away.

A high density altitude takeoff is a delicate balancing act that doesn't tolerate much ham-handed control input; you've got to be gentle, smooth, and willing to fly level at a low altitude for a short while to give the airplane a chance to accelerate to climb speed. This takeoff technique is a lot like the one used for a soft-field departure, in which the pilot induces liftoff at an abnormally low airspeed—in a high density altitude situation, the atmospheric conditions and ground effect do the inducing, and the pilot must respond properly.

Beginning a takeoff roll with more than a mile of runway stretched ahead can be a comforting thing. But put that runway at 7,000 or 8,000 feet above sea level, add just a few degrees of temperature, and it can be downright shocking how quickly all that asphalt moves to the rear.

Sometimes, even in what might be considered mild temperatures, an airport elevation is so high that the takeoff distance goes right off the flight manual's charts. Out-of-towners may quake at the strange, new takeoff distances, and these rarefied strips can give local pilots trouble as well.

> A private pilot and his two passengers escaped injury when their 180-horsepower Piper Arrow crash-landed immediately after takeoff from Reserve, New Mexico. The airport lies at 6,360 feet MSL and given the 55-degree temperature reported at flight time, the density altitude at Reserve was 7,900 feet MSL. Reserve's only runway is 4,800 feet long with rising terrain off both ends.

The maximum density altitude depicted in the Arrow's "Takeoff Distance vs. Density Altitude" chart is 7,000 feet. Although there was no demonstration that the pilot attempted to calculate the plane's takeoff roll, he did prepare a complete weight and balance calculation, which was later submitted to investigators. Maximum operating gross weight for the PA-28R-180 is 2,500 pounds; the accident plane weighed 2,312 pounds, and was within center of gravity limits.

The pilot reported surface winds from 220 degrees at approximately eight to 10 knots and light turbulence at the time of takeoff. He extended the flaps 25 degrees, standard for short-field takeoffs in the Arrow, and departed from Runway 24. Things proceeded normally approximately 100 feet in the air, at which point he retracted the gear and began retracting the flaps.

The Arrow immediately stopped climbing and began to descend. The pilot re-extended the flaps, but to no avail; the rate of descent eased but the airplane continued to sink. The pilot later reported his airspeed was 90 mph, with manifold pressure from 23 to 24 inches and the rpm close to redline. (Sea-level pilots may need to re-orient themselves to the new "takeoff power" numbers they will see at high-altitude airports.)

The pilot located what he termed "fairly clear terrain" among the trees and at 20 feet AGL, cut the power. The landing gear extended automatically, clipped a barbed wire fence and collapsed as the Arrow came to a stop with both wings and underbelly severely damaged. The pilot and his passengers exited unharmed.

In a post-accident statement to investigators, the pilot said he believed he had encountered a downdraft or wind shear at 100 feet AGL which prevented the Arrow from climbing any higher. He cited a witness's report that an extremely strong gust of wind had swept the airport area from the southeast immediately after the airplane left the ground.

The NTSB, however, felt the primary cause was the pilot's inability to maintain altitude, although it accepted the reported downdraft as a factor—in addition to the extremely high density altitude.

But don't forget the aerodynamics involved; when this pilot got that sinking feeling and retracted the flaps, he dumped a lot of lift, and the angle of attack had to be suddenly and significantly increased. That, of course, added a lot of drag, and there was nothing left for the airplane to do but sink even more. With 100 feet of altitude, retracting the landing gear was a good move—that gets rid of drag—but perhaps if the pilot had flown level until the airspeed increased to a comfortable value *then* pulled in the flaps, the Arrow may have had enough energy to overcome the downdraft. Be gentle, be smooth, and don't be in a hurry.

Lacking this finesse with the airplane, you could get yourself into trouble at an airport like Angel Fire. At an elevation 8,382 feet, it lies midway up a narrow valley in the Sangre de Cristo Mountains of northern New Mexico. The airport is so high that the traffic pattern is flown at 11,002 MSL. Angel Fire's one runway is 6,700 feet long and runs lengthwise up the valley, which is defined by mountains ranging up to 13,000 feet. The airport presents enough of a density altitude problem so that a warning is issued in the AOPA's airport directory: "Very high density altitude in summer."

On a May afternoon, an ATP/CFII and his three passengers made it to 300 feet AGL and a half-mile beyond the runway before his Arrow III ran out of air. The instructor was in the right front seat, providing dual to a commercial trainee. Conditions at flight time were VFR with visibility of 30 miles and calm winds, and a temperature of 61 degrees. That's not particularly hot, but when the temperature was applied to the pressure altitude, the density altitude was 10,400 feet—that's high for a fully loaded Cherokee.

The PIC reported that he did a complete preflight using the owner's manual, including calculations of weight and balance and takeoff distance, and determined that his best rate of climb off the runway that day would be 500 feet per minute. (These calculations were made despite the fact that the maximum density altitude on the "Takeoff vs. Density Altitude" chart in the Arrow III handbook is 7,000 feet.) Using the same charts, investigators determined that the Arrow III's best rate of climb that day would have been only 350 feet per minute.

Because his student was unfamiliar with the airplane, the instructor helped with the takeoff; he leaned the mixture, and extended the flaps 10 degrees. The Arrow rotated about two-thirds of the way down the runway. After climbing out of ground effect, the instructor raised the gear, retracted the flaps, and the plane accelerated to 90 knots.

At 300 feet AGL, the Arrow "encountered unexpected turbulence" and promptly quit climbing. The instructor assumed control, but was unable to halt the sink or the decreasing airspeed, which was now down to about 70 knots. He spotted a clearing and turned toward it, was able to lower the gear and straighten the airplane for a flare, stall warning sounding all the time.

A fence sheared the Arrow's landing gear, and on impact a fire erupted in the right fuel tank. The airplane skidded straight ahead for roughly 200 yards. When it came to a stop, the fire in the right wing broke out in earnest, and the four occupants were able to exit through the blown left window.

Six weeks later, a private pilot in a Cherokee 180 tackled Angel Fire from the other direction. VFR conditions prevailed with 50-mile visibility and calm wind. The temperature was 65 degrees, which translated to a density altitude of 10,609 feet.

The pilot stated that he rotated the airplane and was climbing at about 95 mph. He gained an altitude of 200 feet when, he reported, a gust of wind hit the Cherokee from approximately 200 degrees, blowing the airplane sideways and down about 75 feet. The pilot was unable to stop the descent and shortly thereafter flew into the ground. He escaped unhurt while his wife sustained minor injuries. The Cherokee was extensively damaged, with sheared landing gear and damaged wings, prop, and underbelly.

"If I had known the wind was blowing at that altitude,

I would not have taken off," the pilot later reported. "The wind was calm on the runway. After I got into the situation, if I could have gotten more speed I could have recovered. Altitude and wind prevented me from doing this."

It is interesting to note that the pilots in these two accidents stated that they would have been fine if it weren't for the winds they unexpectedly encountered a few hundred feet above the runway. This may underline the special hazards of mountain airports, which include winds that vary greatly with altitude, as well as the obvious density altitude dilemma the pilot faces, with no help from his airplane flight manual. But wait a minute—shouldn't there be a message in a flight manual that stops providing takeoff data 3,000 feet short of the density altitude at which you're operating?

We've emphasized gentle, smooth control technique, and that lengthens the time required to achieve the desired pitch attitudes. While you're being gentle and smooth, the airplane is moving across the ground, and the end result is an inevitable increase in takeoff distance. That's why it is so important to add a big fudge factor to your calculations for takeoff when density altitude is high. Plan long, then add some more, be ready to and willing to reject the takeoff if it doesn't feel right—and when you're committed to fly, do so gently and smoothly.

When a Normal Takeoff
Becomes a *Long* Normal Takeoff

All aircraft performance values are predicated on a machine that is clean aerodynamically (no excessive control gaps, wheel-well doors tightly fitted, controls rigged properly, etc.) and powered by an engine or two in good condition and properly set up (throttle travel what it should be, mixture set correctly, prop governor adjusted and so on). These are things over which the pilot has little or no control at the time of takeoff. Unless there are gross problems present, performance should be reasonably close to the book values.

There are also conditions that, while not under your direct control, must be factored into the calculations that determine whether there's enough runway to contain the upcoming takeoff. Next time you're browsing through the takeoff performance charts for your airplane, notice that all the figures are based on departing from a hard-surfaced, level, dry runway with no wind blowing. All charts provide for the influence of wind, and in most cases, manufacturers publish reduction factors for some of the other conditions mentioned above; almost none of the lightplane handbooks speak to runway slope because it's insignificant unless the runway is a real ski jump, and also because values for runway gradient are seldom published for airports not served by airline operators (gradient gets very significant for big airplanes).

A recently certificated private pilot, his uncle, and a passenger were on a mid-winter trip from Riverside, California, to Denver in a rented Cherokee Arrow IV. The pilot had just completed a thorough checkout in the airplane, but this was to be his first long cross-country flight. His uncle, a private pilot with 2,650 hours and a multi-engine rating was completely inexperienced in this make and model.

They departed Riverside, stopped at Yuma, Arizona, to refuel and according to one account, elected to land at Dove Creek, Colorado, that afternoon for a pit stop. The pilots agreed after two passes over the field that the 4,000-foot strip looked "normal," but when they touched down, they discovered it was a dirt runway that had turned to mud in the afternoon sun. The landing roll transferred a considerable amount of mud from runway to airplane.

The local FBO said it would be wise for them to spend the night, because the mud would be frozen in the morning. They took the FBO's advice, and the next morning a mechanic helped with a heater, rags and deice fluid as they cleaned up the wings and fuselage, and filled the fuel tanks. The FBO also mentioned that the northbound takeoff would be "slightly uphill."

The elevation at Dove Creek is 6,975 feet. The pilots calculated the takeoff performance and reckoned they would be airborne in 2,000 feet and would climb at 270 feet a minute. While even this climb rate is marginal, it appears the pilots did not account for the initial climb rate with gear down, which would be substantially less, according to the Arrow IV handbook.

From the younger pilot's account of the takeoff: "Aircraft rotated at estimated speed and distance, but slightly heavy. On liftoff, about 10 feet above runway, the aircraft drifted to the left. My uncle advised of drift. I started adding more rudder, but no response. My uncle, with my consent, took control. Aircraft wheels met the road at the end of runway. The aircraft bounced across the road into an open field on the other side of the road. My uncle cut the engine and cut switches. The gear collapsed and aircraft slid to a stop, where I cut fuel. Everyone immediately exited."

The uncle had a different story: "At 10 feet above runway, aircraft began drift to left. Undersigned advised PIC, who replied he was 'working on it.' Left drift continued toward low mound, collision with which would have undoubtedly resulted in fatal accident. Undersigned, with consent of PIC, took controls. The aircraft was heavy and non-responsive. Undersigned raised left wing with aileron and heavy rudder to avoid mound to left. Plane 'mushed'; wheels made contact with road at end of runway. In summary, an emergency situation arose which was not created by the PIC or myself in which the PIC was justified in turning over control to the more experienced accompanying pilot. The actions taken were justified and avoided a more serious, if not fatal, accident."

NTSB investigators had a little trouble at first sorting out the question of pilot in command, since the uncle took the title when the accident was first reported. But it developed that the uncle had no time in command of an Arrow, nor any flying time at all in the previous three months. So much for that.

PIC status notwithstanding, whichever pilot accomplished the preflight planning and checked the aircraft loading didn't do a very good job. With full fuel, three people and their baggage, the Arrow was 38 pounds over its maximum gross weight, in addition to the problems of the uphill, crosswind takeoff (pilots of the T-tailed Arrow IV tell us the plane sometimes runs out of rudder in a strong crosswind). Compound the situation with a 7,000-foot field elevation, and one would have to conclude that off-loading of fuel or people should have been considered, even at 20 degrees Fahrenheit, the air temperature at takeoff. The NTSB cited the younger pilot's "inadequate preflight planning" as the probable cause, which is as it should be.

The Effect of Wind

Anyone who has been around flying for more than ten minutes realizes that pilots always take off and land into the wind. We're not alone in that area because birds do the same thing, and for the same reason; wings begin to produce lift as soon as air begins moving over them, and that's a bonus whether you're going or coming.

All takeoff performance charts have provisions for wind effect; Cessna prefers to use a convenient percentage for each 9-knot increment of headwind (Figure 3-1), Beech elected to include wind effect as a column in the chart (Figure 3-2), and Piper shows headwinds as part of the graphic presentation (Figure 3-3). Whichever method is used, the results are the same, and the wind-effect portion of these charts (rather exemplar of the light-plane fleet) can be used as is, except for the realization that some estimation is necessary; all of the charts refer to "headwind" or "wind component down runway."

When the wind is blowing right down the centerline it's all headwind, and every knot can be applied to the no-wind distance to reduce it. But whenever the wind direction is *not* down the runway—and that's just about all the time—the headwind component suffers. You can make an educated guess—this table shows the decrease in headwind component for a 20-knot wind blowing at progressively greater angles to the runway:

Crosswind Angle	Headwind Component
0°	20 kts.
10°	20 kts.
20°	19 kts.
30°	17 kts.
45°	14 kts.
60°	10 kts.
70°	7 kts.
80°	3 kts.
90°	0 kts.

Which might lead you to believe that a direct crosswind will have no effect on takeoff performance, regardless of velocity. But *au contraire*—that wind is now all crosswind component, and all 20 knots is trying to push the airplane off the runway during the ground roll portion of the takeoff. Your counteraction with aileron and rudder will exact a toll in drag and asymmetrical lift production, and takeoff distance will be inexorably increased. How much? Another educated guess is in order, and the wise pilot once again cranks in a big fudge factor; this pilot is also ready and willing to abort the takeoff if it appears necessary.

Downwind takeoffs? Not always an ingredient for disaster, but marginal at best, and attempting one from a lake, in an amphibian, during a thunderstorm, in rough water, adds enough other factors to make a crash much more likely. The pilot of a Lake LA-4-200 Buccaneer found this to be so when he attempted a downwind takeoff from Canyon Lake, Texas, and ended up in the trees. The airplane was destroyed, but the pilot escaped injury.

> In anticipation of the flight, the pilot—a 12,000-hour veteran—had obtained a weather briefing at about 8 that morning. He was informed that there could be thunderstorms in the Canyon Lake area at about the time he expected to arrive, but other than this, the forecast called for VFR conditions throughout the area. The wind was blowing from 150 degrees at 15 knots.
>
> When he arrived over Canyon Lake he could see the thunderstorms to the west and southwest of the lake.
>
> He found some sheltered water on the west side of the lake, landed there without incident and taxied down the shoreline, looking for a place to beach the amphibian. But wind from the approaching thunderstorms had begun to roughen the waters, and the pilot decided to get out while the getting was possible. He took off to the east, away from the storms, and searched for a better location, encountering shifting winds and turbulence during this hop.
>
> A sheltered cove on the northeast side of the lake offered a safe haven, and he landed, noticing that the main body of the lake was now developing whitecaps as the winds got stronger. As he taxied through the rough water on the way to the cove, the left pontoon began to submerge. He even-

tually found he could not keep it out of the water, making another takeoff impossible. He started searching for some-place either to beach the Lake or at least to pull it up far enough to drain the pontoon.

West of the cove he had landed in, he found some sheltered water and a boat ramp, so he taxied out of the water to the top of the boat ramp and after draining the pontoon, rolled back down the ramp to try another takeoff. The pilot had about 3,000 feet of usable water in the cove, and he elected a northwest takeoff to avoid the approaching thunderstorms. His accident report picks up the action:

"Started normal takeoff run. Airplane airborne in about 900 to 1,000 feet. At lift-off, airplane unable to climb and sustain flying altitude. Went back to surface and takeoff run continued with increasing speed ready for liftoff, rotation, and climb over obstacles. Unable to get off and stay off water surface for continued flight. Airplane had occasional heavy overloaded feeling as takeoff run continued."

The Lake ran out of lake and the takeoff came to an abrupt halt in the trees at the far end of the cove. The pilot emerged unscathed.

The pilot noted in his report that perhaps the engine was not functioning up to par. Another pilot (also a mechanic) who witnessed the event agreed. In a short statement at the end of the pilot's account, this witness stated, "I heard the run-up and takeoff run. The engine sounded good at first, and as the takeoff run continued, seemed to be losing power progressively and a very pronounced 'popping' developed in the exhaust—like water in fuel or a wet ignition possibly."

NTSB investigators found no problems with the engine. The probable cause was laid to the downwind takeoff and the approaching thunderstorm instead. Contributing factors were the pilot's failure to abort the takeoff and his failure to gain enough altitude to clear the trees.

To Flap or Not to Flap, That's the Question

We've presented several accident scenarios in which various wing flap settings seemed to play an important part in the outcome. There's a rather common misconception about flaps and takeoff performance, something like "if these flaps do so much for me on landing, they will probably make a positive difference on takeoff as well." But aerodynamics must be considered, for when wing flaps are used during an approach, the airplane is decelerating or flying at a constant airspeed, and during takeoff, flaps can only impede the acceleration, which we've seen is vital to success.

So, why do some manufacturers suggest partial-flap takeoffs? Because the designers have theorized and flight testing has proved that certain airplanes achieve optimum takeoff performance with flaps extended; others do better with no flaps. It doesn't seem "right smart" to swim upstream in this regard, especially when there are absolutely no performance figures to rely on for making the go/no-go decision.

Maximum Performance Takeoffs: Short- and Soft-field Procedures

There seem to be two schools of thought among the manufacturers when it comes to short-field takeoffs; those whose normal takeoff procedures produce maximum performance, and those who publish short-field takeoff procedures that squeeze a little more performance out of the airplane. It doesn't matter in which school your airplane resides, because you're stuck with whatever procedure—and the resultant takeoff distance—that's in the POH. Trying to improve "normal" takeoff distances by using your own airspeeds or flap settings is playing with dynamite; operations outside the approved performance envelope must be left to the professional test pilots. You're not being paid enough to shoulder that kind of responsibility.

Given a fixed amount of available power, takeoff performance can only be enhanced by increasing lift production at low speed or sacrificing long-term climb gradient for early lift-off—or, in most cases, both.

Figure 3-5 is a typical maximum-performance takeoff chart for a light single-engine airplane; compare the no-wind/sea level/23-degree distance over a 50-foot obstacle to the "normal" takeoff performance for the same airplane (Figure 3-2). The max-performance procedure cuts 300 feet off the distance, and it's accomplished with 15 degrees of flap and an airspeed a couple of knots lower than normal.

Notice that the normal procedure calls for lift-off at 70 knots and

Figure 3-5

OBSTACLE TAKE-OFF DISTANCES

ASSOCIATED CONDITIONS

POWER	2700 RPM, FULL THROTTLE
FLAPS	15°
GEAR	RETRACT AFTER LIFT-OFF
RUNWAY	PAVED, LEVEL, DRY SURFACE
WEIGHT	2750 LBS
TAKE-OFF SPEED	78 MPH/68 KTS IAS (MAINTAIN UNTIL CLEAR OF OBSTACLES)

NOTE

FOR EACH 100 POUNDS BELOW 2750 LBS, REDUCE TABULATED DISTANCES BY 8% AND TAKE-OFF SPEEDS BY 1 MPH

WIND COMPONENT DOWN RUNWAY KNOTS	SEA LEVEL			2000 FEET			4000 FEET			6000 FEET			8000 FEET		
	OAT °F	GROUND ROLL FEET	TOTAL OVER 50 FT OBSTACLE FEET	OAT °F	GROUND ROLL FEET	TOTAL OVER 50 FT OBSTACLE FEET	OAT °F	GROUND ROLL FEET	TOTAL OVER 50 FT OBSTACL FEET	OAT °F	GROUND ROLL FEET	TOTAL OVER 50 FT OBSTACLE FEET	OAT °F	GROUND ROLL FEET	TOTAL OVER 50 FT OBSTACLE FEET
0	23	942	1410	16	1104	1643	9	1297	1920	2	1526	2247	-6	1799	2637
	41	1020	1518	34	1196	1771	27	1407	2072	20	1657	2428	13	1956	2852
	59	1100	1630	52	1292	1904	45	1521	2231	38	1793	2617	31	2120	3077
	77	1184	1746	70	1391	2042	63	1640	2395	56	1936	2812	49	2291	3310
	95	1271	1867	88	1495	2185	81	1764	2565	74	2084	3015	67	2469	3553
15	23	820	1214	16	958	1419	9	1123	1663	2	1319	1953	-6	1553	2299
	41	888	1309	34	1040	1532	27	1220	1798	20	1434	2113	13	1690	2490
	59	959	1407	52	1124	1649	45	1322	1939	38	1555	2281	31	1834	2690
	77	1034	1510	70	1213	1771	63	1427	2084	56	1681	2454	49	1985	2898
	95	1112	1617	88	1305	1898	81	1537	2235	74	1812	2635	67	2142	3115
30	23	687	1017	16	806	1194	9	950	1406	2	1120	1658	-6	1324	1960
	41	746	1099	34	877	1292	27	1034	1523	20	1220	1798	13	1444	2127
	59	807	1184	52	951	1394	45	1122	1646	38	1326	1944	31	1570	2303
	77	886	1273	70	1027	1500	63	1214	1772	56	1435	2095	49	1703	2486
	95	939	1366	88	1107	1610	81	1309	1904	74	1550	2254	67	1841	2677

WARNING: Obstacle take off is not a recommended procedure, as it utilizes speeds at or below power-off stall speed. In the event of engine failure or wind speed fluctuations, a stall may occur which may cause uncontrolled contact with the ground.

an acceleration to 73 knots in the first 50 feet of climb; the short-field procedure requires lift-off and climb at 68 knots. That's test-pilot flying, or at least the sort of accuracy achieved only with a lot of practice, which you probably won't have accomplished just prior to a maximum-effort takeoff. To make the numbers come true, you must begin the rotation so that liftoff occurs at precisely the published airspeed, and you must continue the rotation so that the airspeed is maintained at that value until the obstacle is cleared. Neither of these are easy tasks; they require a great deal of proficiency and an intimate knowledge of the airplane's characteristics.

When wing flaps are used to enhance lift production at low airspeed, they need to be retracted for the most efficient normal climbout, but don't be in a rush to clean up the airplane. Climb clear of the obstacles, then nose over a bit and let the airspeed build to a value safely above flaps-up stall speed and then retract the flaps—slowly.

A maximum-performance takeoff puts you a bit on the edge, and you should expect trouble if the engine falters. Of course, there's always trouble when the only engine quits right after takeoff, but at the relatively low airspeeds used for a short-field operation, there will be less time to react. Don't leave Figure 3-5 without reading the warning printed across the bottom; it could be applied to a maximum-performance takeoff in just about any airplane, so perhaps you should think twice about attempting a short-field procedure when success depends on achieving the published values.

How Soft is "Soft?"

Up until this point, every takeoff performance chart or table has referenced a "paved, dry, level runway"—but that's not always the case. There's an obvious benefit to taking off downhill on a sloping runway, but you'll not find any way to quantify that (or the negative effect of an uphill departure) in the POHs for light airplanes. A calm day presents a common-sense solution—always take off downhill—but what about the situation when the wind is blowing up the hill, or vice versa? Without a chart to validate the combination of effects, good luck; you might consider waiting for the wind to change if runway length is critical.

The more likely circumstance is a takeoff from an unpaved

airfield, in which case the type of surface and its condition will certainly lengthen the takeoff ground roll. The big question is, how much? Does the drag of a grass runway increase normal values by 10 percent? 15 percent? 100 percent? The variables go on *ad infinitum,* and there is absolutely no reliable way to calculate the increase.

More Runway Considerations

Notice that Cessna recommends an increase of 15 percent of the ground roll distance for a dry grass runway takeoff in a Skylane (Figure 3-1); but that definition introduces a couple of values that can't be measured—length and type of the grass, and how dry is dry? The pilot is left with no choice but to add that big fudge factor again, and be ready to abort the takeoff if it doesn't feel right.

> Witnesses said that the pilot of a Piper Lance had decided to depart from the south end of a 1,931-foot private grass strip. The strip was covered with damp, 6-inch-tall grass. The Lance left tire tracks that indicated the pilot had turned around short of the end, giving away 284 feet, and leaving only about 1,650 feet for the takeoff.
>
> The Lance lifted off about 1,300 feet after starting its takeoff, and did not appear to climb normally. It was heading directly for a 32-foot water tank located 197 feet from the end of the runway and on the extended centerline. The pilot banked to the right to avoid the tower and cleared a shop building by only a few feet, then banked to the left and struck two power lines. It hit the ground, cartwheeled and crashed.
>
> Investigators noted that the Lance was within 12 pounds of its maximum allowable gross weight at takeoff. The temperature was 93 degrees, making for a density altitude of approximately 2,845 feet, and there was no wind.

Heavy load, hot day, short runway, wet grass, no wind. Put all these together and the calculated takeoff distance may well have been greater than runway available, and the grassy surface—even if it had been dry—added an unknown value to the conditions.

When you don't know, don't go. Given the possible outcome, takeoff is not a good time to go on a guess.

Decisions, Always Decisions

There are some decisions that can really test the judgment of a pilot. One is the decision to go around; another, and more difficult, is the decision to abort a takeoff. It's hard to tell how close one really is to the end of the runway in the best of circumstances, and if complicating factors like flying out of an unfamiliar airport or an unexpected wind shift are added to the decision, the picture can become cloudy to the extent that a pilot might easily make the wrong choice and wind up in the trees.

Exactly that situation occurred in Chestertown, Maryland, when a 20,000-hour CFII elected to continue a takeoff from an unfamiliar grass strip after the wind had unexpectedly shifted; he never made it out of ground effect. Fortunately, neither he or his passenger were injured when the Beech C24R Sierra crashed off the departure end of the runway.

The pilot departed Martin State Airport in Baltimore that afternoon to pick up a passenger at Flying Acres, a grass strip in Chestertown; this was his first trip to the airfield. He planned to ferry the airplane and passenger directly back to Martin State.

He circled the 2,500-foot strip before landing, noting that there was no wind sock, and that the grass had been mowed recently. No unicom service was available, but the pilot determined that the wind was light and variable. He landed to the south, and got the impression of a right tailwind; the aircraft seemed to float, and required a definite crab angle to remain aligned with the runway. The strip had a slight slope, going downhill north to south.

The pilot chose to keep the engine running so he wouldn't have any hot-start problems. The passenger boarded and off they went; the pilot observed the movement of tree leaves and grass around the airfield, and concluded that there was now a light breeze from the north, so he planned his takeoff in that direction.

Aware that the Sierra is a marginal short-field airplane,

and that the turf would add drag during the takeoff roll, he
intended making a trial run to check acceleration, but at
about mid-field the airplane felt ready to fly, so he elected
to continue with the takeoff. However, the Beech did not lift
off until it had traveled about 80 percent of the way down
the runway. It lifted off just at stall speed.

The airplane neither accelerated or climbed. It stayed in
ground effect, traveling down the remainder of the runway
at full power until it ran into a small tree at the north end
of the field under full power. The impact sent the aircraft
careening out of control, and it flopped back to the ground
past the tree, breaking off the nosegear.

After securing the fuel system and electrical switches
and getting out of the airplane, the pilot noticed that the
wind had shifted and was blowing out of the south at about
five knots. He wrote (in his part of the NTSB report) that
this was undoubtedly a factor in the accident, and also cited
urgency and stress (get-home-itis!) because of reports of
thunderstorm activity near Baltimore.

The pilot's recommendations on how to avoid this type of accident
contain some good thoughts: "Avoid situations wherein marginal
runway length is a factor. Add a large 'fudge factor' to the performance data, as soil firmness, drag of turf, wind shifts, and runway
slope are impossible to predict and difficult to judge."

Doing It Right

There is, however, a procedure that will minimize the time spent
dragging the tires through the grass, or rolling sluggishly through
soft dirt. It's a matter of using ground effect to your advantage, and
the objective of a soft-field takeoff is quite simple; get the airplane
into the air as quickly as possible.

When you can do it, taxi onto the takeoff surface as fast as you
are able, and keep right on going; any speed at this point is like
money in the bank, in consideration of the slow acceleration you'll
experience on a soft field. Use the flap setting that is recommended
in the POH, and as soon as the elevator control comes alive, pull the
nose up enough to get the nose wheel off the ground and keep it
there. At this high angle of attack you are not only cutting down tire

drag by one-third, you are also setting the airplane up for unsticking—leaving the ground—at the lowest possible airspeed.

This low-speed lift-off is enhanced by ground effect, and as soon as the mains come out of the grass, lower the nose a bit—not enough to permit a descent, but enough to stop the climb and allow airspeed to build up *in ground effect*. This acceleration is the heart of a successful soft-field takeoff, and it's a touchy procedure; you must balance pitch attitude, airspeed, and the small distance between you and the ground. Think of it as riding along on a bubble of air, constantly moving toward the leading edge. When you get there, airspeed should be at a value that will permit a normal climbout.

Attempting a soft-field takeoff from a short field is a dicey affair; with no accurate guidelines for takeoff distance, you're in the guessing business, and there's little room for error.

In any of these questionable maximum-performance circumstances, there's one factor over which the pilot has complete control, and it's a factor that may have more to do with a successful operation than anything else; we're speaking of aircraft weight. You can always off-load passengers or cargo and come back to pick them up later, you can always defuel. There's always something that doesn't have to go on this trip. Check the charts; there's a significant difference in performance for lighter airplanes.

Up, Up and Away

Airspeed is the foundation of normal climb performance When a pilot does a good job of maintaining the proper airspeed, rate of climb will be determined by weight, density altitude and engine condition. The POH for most single-engine airplanes will provide three climb airspeeds; best angle, best rate, and cruise climb. "Best angle" is the lowest, and provides the greatest gain of altitude per unit of distance; "best rate" is slightly higher, and generates the greatest gain of altitude per unit of time. "Cruise climb" or "normal" climb airspeed is usually a compromise of over-the-nose visibility, engine cooling, and time-to-climb.

As you consider larger airplanes, with the capability of climbing to high altitudes, a climb-speed schedule becomes important. Maintenance of a constant indicated airspeed throughout an extended climb produces an ever-increasing true airspeed, a situation that results in covering a lot of ground in the climb, but that also cuts down the time available to cruise at the more efficient higher altitudes. The POH for such an airplane will provide a schedule in the form of lower indicated airspeeds as you climb, usually in 5,000-foot increments. Following the schedule will get you to cruise altitude as rapidly as possible, which means you can enjoy the benefits longer.

This principle is especially applicable to turbine-powered airplanes, because at high altitudes true airspeed gets very high and fuel flow gets very low. Most turbine pilots will get as high as they can as quickly as they can and stay there as long as they can.

The flight manual graphs or charts on "Normal Climb" are usually close to reality; hold the proper indicated airspeed and you should see climb rates close to book values. A low-time engine should provide nearly the same excess power—that's what determines climb rate—as the test pilot had. Got 1,500 hours on your engine? Better add about 10 percent to the time to climb if compression checks are getting a little weak. Bumpy air? Night? IFR? Don't count on getting the same performance as the POH advertises—that data was obtained in smooth air in daylight with good visual horizon conditions.

Climb rate is one thing; climb gradient is something else, and it's vitally important when you're concerned about climbing over an obstacle in your path—like a mountain range or an antenna farm off the end of the runway. Climb rates are provided in terms of feet per *minute,* but obstacle clearance must be considered in terms of feet per *mile,* so groundspeed must be considered.

For illustration, an airplane climbing in no wind at an airspeed of 60 knots (one mile per minute) and showing a vertical speed of 500 feet per minute is producing a climb gradient of 500 feet per mile. But if the pilot were to double the groundspeed (unlikely, but convenient for this example) and continue climbing at 500 fpm, the climb gradient would drop drastically—only 250 feet per mile. If you think that's not so bad, imagine taking off from your local airport some day and fly for a mile, but be careful not to gain more than 250 feet of altitude; you would get an uncomfortably close view of everything on the ground—and everything sticking up from the ground—in that mile.

Instrument pilots are sometimes tasked with insuring that

their airplanes are able to make good a specified climb gradient in order to guarantee obstacle clearance while climbing in the clouds to an en route altitude. The clue to this requirement will be a note in the IFR Departure section of an approach procedure chart; for example, "Minimum climb of 246 feet per mile required for this departure." The calculation is not difficult; divide climb rate (feet per minute) by groundspeed expressed in miles per minute, and the result is your climb gradient in feet per mile. If it comes out less than the charted requirement, go to Plan B. Don't attempt the departure, because there are usually rocks in those clouds.

Engine Performance

Reciprocating engines—even the very best of them—represent an awkward and inefficient way to convert gasoline's energy to thrust. That assessment is offered with absolutely no intent to offend the aircraft engine manufacturers, because they have done a good job of designing and building the powerplants that keep most of the general aviation fleet aloft. Rather, it's an acknowledgment of the economic restraints that prevent all of us from flying behind turbine engines; a much better way to go, but also a much more expensive way.

Because there is little hope for a technological or economic miracle that will provide small turbine engines at a reasonable cost, we'll be flying recips in light airplanes for a lot of years. There are operational decisions to be made and techniques to be applied that will not only extend the lives of aircraft engines, but can also make them more efficient and reliable.

Engines Were Meant to be Used Often

Fifty miles northeast of Atlanta one starry night, a Piper Aerostar 700 (that's the racer of the Aerostar family, with 350 horsepower on each side) was cruising at 8,500 feet, bound for its home base, a small airport about 30 miles south of Hartsfield International. That's not much altitude for this high-performance machine, but it was a short flight, and the pilot was aware that the airplane had been squawked for low oil pressure and high engine temperatures on several previous flights; he was returning the airplane for maintenance after completing his appointed rounds for the night.

About the time the Aerostar was abeam the Hartsfield Airport, the pilot noticed that the oil pressure on the right engine had dropped to near zero, and the cylinder head and oil temperatures were rising rapidly. No passengers, no cargo, not a lot of fuel on board, so the pilot feathered the right prop and continued toward home.

That in itself was a good decision (there was not much choice, really, because when the oil supply is depleted, the prop will feather anyway), but unfortunately the left alternator failed shortly thereafter. The Aerostar's landing gear and wing flaps require considerable electrical power for extension, and by the time the pilot got the airplane configured for landing, the juice was all gone, the lights went out, and the airplane ran off the end of the runway. The Aerostar was totaled, but the pilot was not hurt.

So, what does an apparent oil-related engine failure have to do with engine performance? A lot in this case, because this particular Aerostar had sat unused at a southeastern airport for several months, never saw the inside of a hangar, never got into the air— as a matter of fact, the engines were never started during this period of time. With absolutely no protection against the elements, the insides of the engine became badly pitted, to the point where people who knew whereof they spoke suggested strongly that the airplane not be flown until the engines were repaired or replaced. The advice was ignored, and the price was paid.

Bad things happen to any engine that sits unused for long periods of time. The film of oil that normally coats interior surfaces drains away and exposes those surfaces to rust and corrosion; condensation provides ample moisture to do a number on the unprotected metal. Some of that water gets into the oil, and the acids that result from the chemical combination obviously do the engine innards no good at all.

There are two ways to prevent this kind of damage; "mothball" the engine (terms like "pickle" and "cocoon" mean roughly the same thing), or operate it on a regular, frequent basis. The former method, of course, is intended only for long-term storage, and must be performed by a shop knowledgeable in the process; this involves treating interior surfaces with special oils, then actually sealing the engine so that no moisture or other contaminants can enter.

Engine manufacturers generally consider 20 hours of flight time per month is required to see an aircraft engine to TBO—that's 20 hours of *flight time* in order to get engine temperatures up to a level that will get rid of moisture and other contaminants. If your schedule simply doesn't permit that kind of regular flying, consider flying the airplane for at least 30 minutes or so each week; it's important to keep the water boiled out of the oil, if nothing else. (There's an obvious concomitant benefit in the matter of pilot currency and proficiency, too!)

Cessna refers to "Flyable Storage" in the Handling, Service & Maintenance section of the POH for the 172: "Airplanes placed in non-operational storage for a maximum of 30 days...are considered in flyable storage status. Every seventh day during these periods, the propeller should be rotated by hand through five revolutions. This action 'limbers' the oil and prevents any accumulation of corrosion on engine cylinder walls.

"After 30 days [of such storage], the airplane should be flown for 30 minutes or a ground runup should be made just long enough to produce an oil temperature within the lower green arc range. Excessive ground runup should be avoided.

"Engine runup also helps to eliminate excessive accumulations of water in the fuel system and other air spaces in the engine. If the airplane is to be stored temporarily, or indefinitely, refer to the Service Manual for proper storage procedures."

That sort of advice doesn't appear in many POHs, but because all light aircraft engines are essentially alike and the forces of nature don't respect nameplates, it's advice well worth heeding. And to keep the entire machine in good condition, therefore more likely to deliver the performance you expect, we recommend frequent flights over occasional ground runups.

Engine Performance During Takeoff and Climb

Takeoff-distance charts are based on the assumption that the pilot will use full power every time—no exceptions. (No exceptions for reciprocating engines, that is. There are situations in which turbine engines may be "powered down" a bit for takeoff because of low air temperature, but pilots of recips don't have a choice in this regard.) The charts make it very clear, with words such as "Power: 2600 rpm and full throttle before brake release."

As density altitude increases (doesn't matter whether it's the result of high temperature or high airport elevation or a combination thereof), the engine may still provide enough power to turn the prop at the maximum rpm, but there's not as much thrust being developed, and takeoff distance will suffer accordingly. The important point is that the throttle should be opened all the way on every takeoff so that the engine can develop all the power that's available. (Turbocharged engines have manifold pressure limits that can sometimes be exceeded at full throttle, and those limits must be observed.)

The point at which engine power should be reduced from the takeoff setting (maximum available) to climb power (usually something less than maximum) has always been open to individual preference. Given the fact that virtually all light aircraft recips are certificated to run wide open all day long, there's nothing wrong with climbing all the way to cruise altitude at full power. This is, of course, the norm for airplanes with fixed-pitch propellers, but with a constant-speed prop there is some efficiency to be realized by climbing at a lower power setting. It's also easier on the ears and the wallet—fuel burn, you know.

Some pilots prefer to maintain full power to 500 feet AGL, others like 1,000 feet even better, reasoning that if an engine failure is going to occur, it will probably happen at the first power reduction, a long-standing tenet (myth?) of lightplane flying that may or may not have a basis in fact. But if your engine has no power-time limit and you feel better with full power, go right ahead, you'll get where you're going—vertically—faster, and if the engine does quit, there's more altitude to work with, and a better chance of pulling off a successful forced landing.

Pilots of retractable-gear airplanes have one additional consideration. It would be folly to reduce power before the wheels are in the wells, and the general procedure is to hold off gear retraction until there's no more usable runway ahead for landing in the event of engine failure. When the gear comes up, the power should come back if you're comfortable with altitude at that time, and if you intend to climb out at a reduced power setting.

Figure 4-1

TIME, FUEL, AND DISTANCE TO CLIMB

MAXIMUM RATE OF CLIMB

CONDITIONS:
Flaps Up
Full Throttle
Standard Temperature

NOTES:
1. Add 1.1 gallons of fuel for engine start, taxi and takeoff allowance.
2. Mixture leaned above 3000 feet for maximum RPM.
3. Increase time, fuel and distance by 10% for each 10°C above standard temperature.
4. Distances shown are based on zero wind.

WEIGHT LBS	PRESSURE ALTITUDE FT	TEMP °C	CLIMB SPEED KIAS	RATE OF CLIMB FPM	FROM SEA LEVEL		
					TIME MIN	FUEL USED GALLONS	DISTANCE NM
2300	S.L.	15	73	770	0	0.0	0
	1000	13	73	725	1	0.3	2
	2000	11	72	675	3	0.6	3
	3000	9	72	630	4	0.9	5
	4000	7	71	580	6	1.2	8
	5000	5	71	535	8	1.6	10
	6000	3	70	485	10	1.9	12
	7000	1	69	440	12	2.3	15
	8000	-1	69	390	15	2.7	19
	9000	-3	68	345	17	3.2	22
	10,000	-5	68	295	21	3.7	27
	11,000	-7	67	250	24	4.2	32
	12,000	-9	67	200	29	4.9	38

Aircraft climb performance—i.e. time, fuel and distance during the climb—varies with weight, air temperature and airspeed for a specific climb schedule. Manufacturers usually present two climb schedules, one designated "maximum rate of climb," the other "normal" or "cruise climb." Engine power is set at the beginning of the climb, and changes only in response to decreased air density as altitude increases. Therefore, engine performance becomes very important once you have decided on the climb schedule to be followed, and optimum engine performance can only be obtained by proper management of power output.

The secret, of course, is mixture strength, and most climb-performance charts will provide guidance in this respect. For example, the Cessna 172 "Time, Fuel and Distance to Climb" chart (Figure 4-1) indicates that the mixture should be leaned for maximum rpm above 3,000 feet pressure altitude (3,000 feet MSL, for all practical purposes). When you're considering whether it's safe to lean the mixture at any time during a full-power climb, the first place to check is the POH or the engine manufacturer's operating instructions. Keep in mind that all aircraft engines are adjusted to a super-rich mixture strength at full throttle to provide sufficient internal cooling; but as a climb progresses, the power output of a normally aspirated (non-turbocharged) engine decreases, internal temperatures also decrease, and that over-rich mixture is no longer needed. The cut-off point is generally accepted at about 75 percent power, and that usually happens at about 5,000 feet pressure altitude—a good-enough rule of thumb, but look in the book and be sure. (Cessna apparently concluded that the 172 can be safely leaned at a lower altitude.)

A more sophisticated climb chart for a much higher-performance airplane (Figure 4-2) includes the engine rpm, manifold pressure and fuel flow for successive altitude segments during the climb.

Selection of a climb schedule depends mostly on winds aloft and distance to be flown. If there's a real boomer of a tailwind at a reasonable cruise altitude and you've a long trip ahead, the "max climb rate" schedule will get you up to the benefits sooner, and allow you to cruise at a higher groundspeed for a longer period of time. The down side is the amount of fuel burned, and that should be carefully considered.

Figure 4-2

TIME, FUEL, AND DISTANCE TO CLIMB

MAXIMUM RATE OF CLIMB

CONDITIONS:
Flaps Up
Gear Up
2600 RPM
Cowl Flaps Open
Standard Temperature

PRESS ALT	MP	PPH
S.L. to 17,000	37	162
19,000	35	150
21,000	33	138
23,000	31	126

NOTES:
1. Add 16 pounds of fuel for engine start, taxi and takeoff allowance.
2. Increase time, fuel and distance by 10% for each 10°C above standard temperature.
3. Distances shown are based on zero wind.

WEIGHT LBS	PRESS ALT FT	CLIMB SPEED KIAS	RATE OF CLIMB FPM	FROM SEA LEVEL		
				TIME MIN	FUEL USED POUNDS	DISTANCE NM
4000	S.L.	100	930	0	0	0
	4000	100	890	4	12	7
	8000	100	845	9	24	16
	12,000	100	790	14	38	25
	16,000	100	720	19	52	36
	20,000	98	515	26	69	50
	23,000	96	340	33	85	66
3700	S.L.	98	1060	0	0	0
	4000	98	1020	4	10	6
	8000	98	975	8	21	13
	12,000	98	915	12	33	21
	16,000	98	845	17	45	30
	20,000	97	630	22	59	42
	23,000	95	445	28	72	55
3400	S.L.	96	1205	0	0	0
	4000	96	1165	3	9	5
	8000	96	1120	7	19	12
	12,000	96	1060	11	29	18
	16,000	96	985	15	39	26
	20,000	95	760	19	51	36
	23,000	94	565	24	61	46

For example, compare the time, distance and fuel consumption for a 4,000-pound C210 climbing to 16,000 feet: Maximum rate will require 19 minutes and 52 pounds of fuel to travel 36 miles on the way up; the "normal" climb schedule (Figure 4-3) will require nine additional minutes, only seven more pounds of fuel, but the airplane will travel 22 miles farther—wind makes the difference, and you need to put pencil to paper on a flight-by-flight basis to decide which altitude and which schedule is best for today's conditions.

High-Altitude Takeoffs: A Different Ball Game

The takeoff performance charts—ground roll, distance over a 50-foot obstacle, initial climb rate—for any airplane are based on maximum output from the powerplant, and for most airplanes that will be significantly reduced by increases in density altitude. The pilot's primary concern in this regard is to adjust the engine controls so that maximum available power is produced; the type of engine—normally aspirated or turbocharged—makes the difference when it comes to procedure.

Most turbocharged engines are able to maintain full rated horsepower to altitudes higher than any of the airports in the United States, and the performance losses will be mostly aerodynamic—thrust from the prop and lift from the wings. The POH will provide rather specific values for manifold pressure, rpm and fuel flow so that you'll know when maximum power is being produced. Of course, when those instructions are ignored, and a pilot elects to use something that worked on another airplane, he may get into deep trouble.

The airport at Santa Fe, New Mexico, is one that requires attention to density altitude and proper engine operation. Field elevation is 6,344 feet, and at the time of this accident, the air temperature of 83 degrees produced a density altitude of 8,900 feet. The A36 Bonanza—lots of horsepower, but no supercharger—was substantially damaged when it crashed shortly after takeoff. The pilot and his two passengers suffered only minor injuries.

The pilot was unfamiliar with flying in mountainous areas and congested airspace, so he was accompanied by a

Figure 4-3

TIME, FUEL, AND DISTANCE TO CLIMB

NORMAL CLIMB - 110 KIAS

CONDITIONS:
Flaps Up
Gear Up
2500 RPM
33 Inches Hg.
125 PPH Fuel Flow
Cowl Flaps Open
Standard Temperature

NOTES:
1. Add 16 pounds of fuel for engine start, taxi and takeoff allowance.
2. Increase time, fuel and distance by 10% for each 8°C above standard temperature.
3. Distances shown are based on zero wind.

WEIGHT LBS	PRESS ALT FT	RATE OF CLIMB FPM	FROM SEA LEVEL		
			TIME MIN	FUEL USED POUNDS	DISTANCE NM
4000	S.L.	660	0	0	0
	4000	615	6	13	12
	8000	580	13	27	25
	12,000	530	20	42	40
	16,000	480	28	59	58
	20,000	410	37	78	79
3700	S.L.	760	0	0	0
	4000	715	5	11	10
	8000	680	11	23	21
	12,000	630	17	36	34
	16,000	580	24	50	49
	20,000	510	31	65	66
3400	S.L.	875	0	0	0
	4000	830	5	10	9
	8000	795	10	20	18
	12,000	745	15	31	29
	16,000	695	20	43	42
	20,000	620	27	55	56

flight instructor who was acting as safety pilot and giving the pilot pointers.

At 1:30 p.m. (probably the hottest time of day), the pilot got ready for takeoff from Santa Fe; his preparations included leaning the mixture to compensate for the airport's elevation.

Satisfied that everything was in order, the takeoff commenced, but shortly after lift-off, the engine began losing power. The Bonanza could not maintain altitude, and the pilot was forced to land on rough desert terrain.

Post-accident investigation of the spark plugs showed clear signatures of lean-mixture operation, and the CFI confirmed that the pilot had leaned the mixture prior to takeoff. That may be okay for most non-turbo airplanes, but the A36 Bonanza features a variable-output fuel pump that adjusts the flow of gasoline downward as air pressure decreases—an automatic mixture control. When this pilot cut back the fuel even more, the engine could produce only as much power as there was fuel to work with. A classic illustration of not knowing what makes the airplane tick.

Adjusting a non-turbocharged engine for max power is a bit more touchy, and somewhat subjective. POHs may advise you to lean for maximum rpm, or lean until the engine runs smoothly; if a pilot misses the mark a bit on either side, power production may suffer. Suffice it to say that when preparing for a high-altitude takeoff with a normally aspirated engine, it's necessary to open the throttle, then *slowly* lean the mixture control until the tachometer reaches its highest point (you'll have to lean slightly beyond peak rpm in order to find it, then move the control toward rich again to re-establish the peak value). Leave the mixture control in this position throughout the takeoff unless the engine falters, at which signal you should increase the mixture strength just enough to make the engine run smoothly again. If some is good, more is *not* better, because even a slightly over-rich mixture is a significant power thief—and you may not have much to work with going in.

A Cessna 172RG departed a 4,000-foot gravel runway near Albuquerque on a hot September afternoon; air temperature 90 degrees F, altimeter 30.20, field elevation 5,270 feet. On board were two pilots; one being checked out in the airplane, the other a CFI.

From the instructor's report: "The first time I noticed a sluggishness in the aircraft was just before liftoff. The runway is 4,000 feet long, and at liftoff we were committed, there was no way to abort the takeoff. We missed the trees at the runway's end by about ten feet and the engine began to lose power. I took over the controls and turned the plane to the east with the intention of landing on Runway 21. The plane began to lose more power and descend. I had the other pilot check the magnetos for a bad one, but there wasn't a substantial difference, so the magnetos were again put on both. The plane just missed power lines on two occasions and the stall warning horn was going off frequently.

I finally saw that I could make it to Runway 21, but because of a building close to the end of the runway I had to start my turn for landing about a quarter of the way down the 3,600-foot downhill runway. I made a steep bank (35 degrees) for the altitude I was above the ground, and the airspeed I was flying at. I concentrated on keeping the nose down in the turn and maintaining airspeed, but as I came out of the turn and lined up with the runway, I relaxed a little, let the nose come up too much and since the airspeed was low anyway, the airplane stalled about ten feet off the runway. I recognized this and immediately put the nose down to recover, but I had no more speed and the plane dropped like a rock.

Just before the airplane hit the ground, I flared it to try to hit on the mains instead of the nosewheel. The main wheels hit first but the nosewheel then hit extremely hard. The nosewheel tire was busted, the main gear were damaged and the firewall was damaged."

The RG's engine was not so badly damaged that it couldn't be run, and investigators found that the fuel mixture control for the engine was very sensitive. Excessive leaning from the full rich position at full power resulted in a rapid engine power loss. The pilot leaned the mixture for maximum rpm as part of his pre-takeoff procedure, but he did so at a low power setting. There just wasn't enough fuel available to keep the engine running at full throttle.

Engine Performance at Cruise

The variables that affect overall airplane performance—weight, altitude, temperature, airspeed, power setting—must be considered in all the regimes of flight, but the job is less complicated for the cruise portion of a trip. Once established in level flight, pilots tend to adjust the engine controls to obtain a particular power setting and accept whatever airspeed results. That's not all bad, unless it completely stifles any creative thinking that might produce more efficient engine operation in the steady-state environment of cruise flight. Is one power setting best for all circumstances?

In very light, low-powered airplanes, the answer is probably yes, because most of the horses under the hood are required to keep the machine in the air; any significant power reduction (ostensibly to save fuel) may cause such a decrease in airspeed (a combination of less thrust and more induced drag) that the purpose of the exercise is defeated.

For whatever reasons, a cruise power setting of 65 percent has become almost traditional for the four-cylinder, fixed-pitch propeller airplanes, in part because the altitudes at which these aircraft operate most of the time don't permit much more power than that to be developed. The almost-equally traditional engine-speed range—2300-2400 rpm—stops producing 65 percent at about 4,000 feet or so, and many pilots are reluctant to push their engines beyond this speed—whether this stems from concern for engine life or personal comfort (noise, vibration) is immaterial.

The cruise performance chart for the Cessna 172 (Figure 4-4) provides power/airspeed/fuel burn comparisons typical for this class of airplane. For example, at 4,000 feet on a standard day, a power increase from 64 percent to 75 percent generates an additional 8 knots, but at the cost of 1.3 gallons of gasoline per hour—and a lot more noise, if that's one of your concerns. Decision time again; is it worth the extra dollars to travel a mere 8 miles farther each hour? The relatively low true airspeeds of these airplanes means that they will be much more negatively affected by adverse winds; if you can only increase your cruise speed by 8 knots in a 30-

Figure 4-4

CRUISE PERFORMANCE

CONDITIONS:
2300 Pounds
Recommended Lean Mixture

PRESSURE ALTITUDE FT	RPM	20°C BELOW STANDARD TEMP			STANDARD TEMPERATURE			20°C ABOVE STANDARD TEMP		
		% BHP	KTAS	GPH	% BHP	KTAS	GPH	% BHP	KTAS	GPH
2000	2500	- - -	- - -	- - -	75	116	8.4	71	115	7.9
	2400	72	111	8.0	67	111	7.5	63	110	7.1
	2300	64	106	7.1	60	105	6.7	56	105	6.3
	2200	56	101	6.3	53	100	6.1	50	99	5.8
	2100	50	95	5.8	47	94	5.6	45	93	5.4
4000	2550	- - -	- - -	- - -	75	118	8.4	71	118	7.9
	2500	76	116	8.5	71	115	8.0	67	115	7.5
	2400	68	111	7.6	64	110	7.1	60	109	6.7
	2300	60	105	6.8	57	105	6.4	54	104	6.1
	2200	54	100	6.1	51	99	5.9	48	98	5.7
	2100	48	94	5.6	46	93	5.5	44	92	5.3
6000	2600	- - -	- - -	- - -	75	120	8.4	71	120	7.9
	2500	72	116	8.1	67	115	7.6	64	114	7.1
	2400	64	110	7.2	60	109	6.8	57	109	6.4
	2300	57	105	6.5	54	104	6.2	52	103	5.9
	2200	51	99	5.9	49	98	5.7	47	97	5.5
	2100	46	93	5.5	44	92	5.4	42	91	5.2
8000	2650	- - -	- - -	- - -	75	122	8.4	71	122	7.9
	2600	76	120	8.6	71	120	8.0	67	119	7.5
	2500	68	115	7.7	64	114	7.2	60	113	6.8
	2400	61	110	6.9	58	109	6.5	55	108	6.2
	2300	55	104	6.2	52	103	6.0	50	102	5.8
	2200	49	98	5.7	47	97	5.5	45	96	5.4
10,000	2650	76	122	8.5	71	122	8.0	67	121	7.5
	2600	72	120	8.1	68	119	7.6	64	118	7.1
	2500	65	114	7.3	61	114	6.8	58	112	6.5
	2400	58	109	6.5	55	108	6.2	52	107	6.0
	2300	52	103	6.0	50	102	5.8	48	101	5.6
	2200	47	97	5.6	45	96	5.4	44	95	5.3
12,000	2600	68	119	7.7	64	118	7.2	61	117	6.8
	2500	62	114	6.9	58	113	6.5	55	111	6.2
	2400	56	108	6.3	53	107	6.0	51	106	5.8
	2300	50	102	5.8	48	101	5.6	46	100	5.5
	2200	46	96	5.5	44	95	5.4	43	94	5.3

knot headwind, might as well stay at 65 percent and enjoy the scenery.

But in the case of a higher-powered airplane that can generate much higher cruise speeds, even at a 65 percent power setting, the ability to overcome or at least negate relatively strong headwinds augurs well for the selection of different power settings for different circumstances. The big difference, in addition to more raw power, is of course the controllable-pitch propeller. Now, a pilot can select an efficient, quiet engine speed, and adjust the manifold pressure (MAP) to provide the thrust necessary for the speed he wants.

Right away, another decision is required—what MAP should be used with what rpm? There's a general rule of thumb for this, one that none other than the vaunted Charles Lindbergh discovered early in his aviation career. Combining his innate (although uneducated) sense of mechanical engineering and a lot of experience, Lindbergh figured out that the combination of low rpm and high MAP provided the most efficient power setting, especially for long-range cruise—and you'll have to admit that he was the expert in that field for a lot of years.

During his short tour with Air Force fighter pilots in the South Pacific during World War II, Lindy always returned to base with more fuel than anyone else; teaching by example, he soon convinced the others that they didn't need to run their P-38s wide open (which required full rich mixture, of course) all the time. Lindbergh's high-MAP, low-rpm technique extended the combat range of the Lightning by hundreds of miles, undoubtedly saved some pilots from landing in the ocean with empty tanks, and it works just as well in today's airplanes.

The principle is easy to understand: No matter what the engine speed, some of the energy in the fuel is used to overcome internal friction—there are a lot of parts rubbing against each other in there! As engine speed increases, friction increases at a greater rate. Therefore, it makes sense to run the engine at the lowest practical speed, reducing friction loss to a minimum and making more fuel energy available for the production of power.

Selection of the proper combination of engine speed and manifold pressure is founded in a number of considerations; engine structural and temperature limits, noise and vibration, fuel flow and airspeed for example. But pilots are not left to their own

Figure 4-5

POWER SETTING TABLE

MANIFOLD PRESSURE – INCHES MERCURY

PRESS. ALT. FEET	STD. ALT. TEMP. °F	55% POWER					65% POWER					75% POWER				
RPM		2200	2300	2400	2500	2575	2200	2300	2400	2500	2575	2200	2300	2400	2500	2575
S.L.	59	29.0	27.7	26.8	26.0	25.0	32.8	31.1	30.0	29.2	28.2		34.8	33.8	32.8	31.5
2000	52	29.0	27.7	26.8	26.0	25.0	32.8	31.1	30.0	29.2	28.2		34.8	33.8	32.8	31.5
4000	45	29.0	27.7	26.8	26.0	25.0	32.8	31.1	30.0	29.2	28.2		34.8	33.8	32.8	31.5
6000	38	29.0	27.7	26.8	26.0	25.0	32.8	31.1	30.0	29.2	28.2		34.8	33.8	32.8	31.5
8000	31	29.0	27.7	26.8	26.0	25.0		31.1	30.0	29.2	28.2				32.8	31.5
10000	23	29.0	27.7	26.8	26.0	25.0		31.1	30.0	29.2	28.2			33.8	32.8	31.5
12000	16		27.7	26.8	26.0	25.0			30.0	29.2	28.2			33.8	32.8	31.5
14000	9		27.7	26.8	26.0	25.0			30.0	29.2	28.2				32.8	31.5
16000	2			26.8	26.0	25.0				29.2	28.2					31.5
18000	-5				26.0	25.0				29.2	28.2					31.5
20000	-12				26.0	25.0					28.2					31.5

For each 6°F above std. temp. add 0.4" MAP.
For each 6°F below std. temp. subtract 0.4" MAP.

APPROXIMATE FUEL FLOW	
BEST ECONOMY	BEST POWER
55% Power 9.2 GPH	55% Power 11. GPH
65% Power 10.8 GPH	65% Power 12.7 GPH
75% Power 12. GPH	75% Power 14. GPH

NOTE: Fuel flow will vary with altitude; therefore, cruise fuel control must be accomplished by adjusting EGT (peak EGT for best economy and peak EGT plus 100°F rich for best power) rather than leaning to an indicated fuel flow.

devices in this regard; the Pilot's Operating Handbook for every airplane contains rpm/MAP limitations for cruise power settings in one form or another.

Figure 4-5 illustrates cruise power settings in tabular form; for each of three popular percentages of power, the table shows the MAP required at various engine speeds. (Note that power production begins to fall off with altitude at the lower engine speeds, because the turbo depends on exhaust gas energy; 2200 rpm can't produce 75 percent power at any altitude—there isn't enough exhaust energy to spin the turbo fast enough to produce the required manifold pressure.) These MAP values should be considered maximum—operational limitations, as in FAR 91.9—for the respective engine speeds.

As usual, there's more than one way to present operational data, and Figure 4-6 is a typical power-setting graph. There are no manifold pressure values shown, because this is a normally aspirated engine, and all the settings represent a full-throttle condition or the limiting MAP.

For example, if you wished to use 2300 rpm in cruise at 4,000 feet at a power setting of 65 percent, full-throttle MAP would be close to 26 inches (standard sea-level pressure of 29.92 inches minus one inch for each 1,000 feet of altitude). Referring to the Manifold Pressure vs. RPM chart supplied with this airplane (Figure 4-7), it is apparent that 26 inches of manifold pressure would exceed the limit; 24.2 inches is as much pressure as this engine can stand at 2300 rpm. No matter how the information is presented, you'll find a maximum manifold pressure for each engine speed.

The certification rules require that pilots be made aware of fuel consumption rates at the various power settings presented in the charts, and some manufacturers choose to include this information on the power charts; others supply separate charts or graphs for this purpose. Regardless of the type of presentation, there is one value of interest to pilots looking for the most efficient cruise power setting, and that's *specific range*—the number of pounds (or gallons, if you like) per air mile. It's a value you won't find in any lightplane POHs, but it's the only way to make a sensible selection of cruise power, and it's easy to calculate—simply divide fuel flow by true airspeed.

Now you have a value that can be derived for any power setting,

Figure 4-6

CRUISE OPERATION

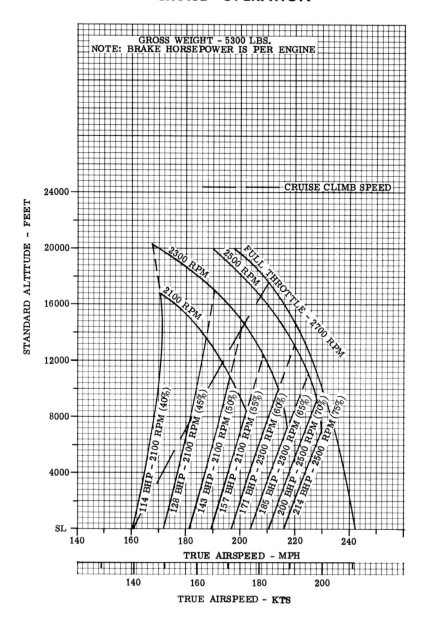

and that can be compared to any other power setting to determine which is more efficient.

Keep firmly in mind that specific range deals in *air miles*—no wind is considered. Don't be fooled into thinking that your airplane has suddenly developed seven-league boots when you find a very efficient power setting; you must always include the wind component in your calculations. A high value for specific range (a lot of air miles for each pound of gasoline) may well be rendered useless in the real world; air miles are eaten up rapidly by strong headwinds.

Chances are that the "Cruise Speed" in the POH is achieved at *maximum cruise power*, and that the "Range" is at *maximum range power*. The two may be 50 knots apart. And chances are that the airplane's "Maximum Payload" (passengers plus baggage) can't be carried for the distance indicated as "Maximum Range," let alone do it at "Maximum Cruise" speed.

Specific range charts covering a variety of airplane weights, altitudes, and ambient temperatures used to show up in military manuals and some POHs, and they were usually in the form of graphs that displayed a family of curves where the peaks represented best "miles-per-gallon." Nowadays, the airspeed value given for "Maximum Range" may be much higher than the real maximum-range airspeed, because the actual value of maximum range airspeed is too low to be marketable. In other words, the "Maximum Cruise," "Economy Cruise," and "Long Range Cruise" AFM data may not be the optimums. The data are probably pretty accurate—any pilot flying in smooth air and using the proper leaning procedure should get close to the book figures—but maybe nowhere near the optimums.

The cruise-performance charts are almost always made out for "no-wind" conditions. Many pilots figure that a 90-degree crosswind en route is the same as no wind. This isn't true. A wind at 90 degrees to the intended course over the ground is a headwind, and it can be a *considerable* headwind if your true airspeed is low and the wind velocity is high. The crosswind correction angle that's required to keep you on course will knock the socks off your groundspeed. Don't count on the AFM to explain this to you. That's basic flying technique, something the manufacturer isn't required to include in the handbook. Break out the E6B computer, set up a wind triangle, and see for yourself what a degradation a crosswind can be.

Figure 4-7

MANIFOLD PRESSURE VS RPM

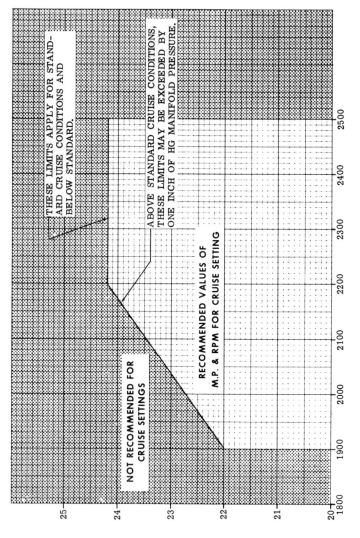

Leaning—Almost an Art Form

We quote from the "Operations Manual" of an 85-horsepower two-seat airplane, circa mid-1940s: "If installed as optional equipment, the mixture control is to be always set at 'full rich' for starting and takeoff purposes. Pulling out on the control leans the fuel mixture. The mixture control is not a device for cutting down fuel consumption, but rather a device for obtaining better engine operation and performance. The mixture control should be used cautiously to lean mixtures to give maximum engine rpm when flying above 5000 feet pressure altitude. Too lean a mixture will cause excessive engine heating and result in damage."

Airplane engines have gotten a lot more complicated over the years, but the principles of mixture control haven't changed a bit since that treatise was written. Unfortunately, "the mixture control should be used cautiously" plus the fact that mixture knobs are red—an obvious warning—has probably led some pilots to conclude that it's easier and safer to leave the mixture control snugged up against the panel all the time. Easier perhaps, but certainly not safer, because fuel consumption can be much higher than book values, which are predicated on proper leaning.

In general, reciprocating aircraft engines are designed to run best on a 14-to-1 ratio of air to fuel—14 parts of air, one part of fuel. But designers recognized the need for something to carry away the excess heat of combustion at full power, and fuel was the answer. As a result, at full throttle and full rich mixture, the fuel-air ratio is changed significantly to provide extra fuel for internal cooling.

It follows that at any power setting less than maximum, when the cooling requirement no longer exists, the mixture will be too rich to provide the optimum 14-to-1 ratio—and engine efficiency drops remarkably. Enter the mixture control, which enables the pilot to adjust the flow of fuel to match the conditions.

Whether you lean using your senses (listening and feeling for roughness, as in most very small airplanes) or by watching the tachometer for maximum rpm, or with an EGT gauge, the principle is the same. You are attempting to find the optimum fuel-air ratio for the amount of power being produced.

As soon as the mixture control is moved toward lean, the ratio begins to improve. Sooner or later, all of the cooling fuel will have been taken away, and all of the energy in the gasoline is being used for power production—if you continue leaning beyond this point, there is no longer enough fuel to support combustion, and the engine begins to run rough and lose power. A slight richening of the mixture—only until the engine runs smoothly again—will result in the proper fuel-air ratio.

That simple method works for simple engines, but the larger ones—particularly those with turbosuperchargers—can run smoothly at rather lean mixture settings, but the exhaust gases will be so hot because of all the power being produced, that exhaust valves and other internal parts may be badly damaged. A more accurate leaning method is needed, and that need is filled by an exhaust-gas temperature sensing system—EGT for short. Now, as excess fuel is removed from the engine and the exhaust gases get hotter, you can see the rise in temperature on a panel instrument; when the EGT reaches its highest value (the "peak," indicating that all the fuel molecules are being burned—no fuel left for cooling), the engine is operating most efficiently.

Leaning with an EGT takes outside air temperature into consideration, and results in a very accurate mixture setting, and a condition often referred to as "best economy." In other words, the engine is now providing the most power per unit of fuel.

Unfortunately, airspeed suffers somewhat in this configuration because some of the fuel energy is being used to overcome internal friction and pumping loss—the energy required to compress the air-fuel mixture in each cylinder during the combustion process. If maximum economy is your goal, you're there; but the price of regaining the "lost" airspeed (usually on the order of 2 percent or so) is a slight increase in fuel consumption, and the additional speed may make the whole operation more efficient in terms of specific range. Once again, it's necessary to put pencil to paper to really figure out what power setting is best for a given situation.

The power charts for larger engines will include special instructions to prevent more heat than the exhaust valves can tolerate. Depending on engine instrumentation, this limitation will be expressed in terms of a lower EGT or increased fuel flow; either way, fuel in excess of that required to support combustion is added for the purpose of internal cooling. There's no such thing as a free lunch. This is known as operating "on the rich side of peak," and the procedure is a simple one; move the mixture control slowly toward lean until the EGT stops rising, continue toward lean to confirm that you've passed the peak temperature, then slowly back toward rich. When the indicator returns to the peak reading, continue adding fuel (mixture control toward rich) until the exhaust gas temperature drops 50 degrees, or 75, or whatever limit the manufacturer has prescribed for that power setting.

The secret of accurate leaning with an EGT gauge is slow, steady pressure on the mixture control as you move it either direction. Temperature is sensed by a special probe that generates a small electrical current in response to heat; it's almost instantaneous, but there's always a slight delay in the indication—just enough to "float" right on by the desired reading unless you stop moving the mixture control a bit ahead of the needle. If you'll think pressure instead of movement, and keep the pressure on until the indicator is almost where is should be (or when it's approaching the peak temperature, evident by a slowdown of needle movement), you will avoid chasing the needle and arrive at the proper setting the first time around.

On occasion, an engine is capable of handling the heat of combustion without extra fuel for cooling. This occurs at low, long-range power settings, and the POH will indicate that leaning to an EGT on the *lean* side of peak is permitted. Now, fuel flow is decreased to the point where excess air is being used for cooling. This is a relatively rare configuration, and "lean side" operation should never be attempted unless the book indicates that it's all right to do so.

Many larger engines need so much extra fuel for cooling at take-off power that the system provides too much fuel even at idle. This is often characterized by "loping" or rough running on the ground, and can be overcome by leaning to smoothness or peak rpm.

Let's Head for the Deck

Engine performance ceases to be a concern during descent...or does it? Given our rather wide-ranging approach to the subject of engine performance (we've been discussing anything that affects efficiency and proper operation), the answer to that question depends on how the descent is conducted and what kind of engine is involved.

For example, the pilot operating with a fixed-pitch propeller may choose to descend by simply pushing the nose over a bit and going downhill at whatever airspeed—and therefore engine speed—results. If no changes are made in throttle position during such a descent, power production will increase as air density builds, and mixture strength will have to be adjusted accordingly. In the extreme, the engine would begin to run rough—might even quit—when the amount of fuel being delivered to the carburetor is insufficient to support combustion at that throttle setting. It's exactly the same as over-leaning—sooner or later, there's just not enough gasoline to keep the fire burning; you'll need to richen the mixture strength periodically during such a descent. The alternative is to go to full rich when you start down, but that wastes fuel and may result in a significant thermal shock as a shot of altitude-cooled fuel enters the engine.

Another procedure involves a decision to descend at or near cruise airspeed—perhaps because of turbulence or plain old pilot preference—and a power reduction is required. Many pilots respond to a concern for running the engine too lean at a lower altitude by pushing the mixture control all the way to full rich when they pull the throttle back for descent. But think this through; if the mixture strength were correct for cruising at say, 65 percent, it should supply plenty of fuel for a lower power setting. Reducing power *and* richening the mixture is a double whammy—wastes fuel and cools the engine, neither of which is desirable. Remember, the only time a small engine needs to be operated at full rich is at power settings greater than 75 percent. And most of them just won't produce 75 percent below 5,000 feet.

Those procedures apply generally to normally aspirated engines, but with a turbocharged powerplant, manifold pressure will remain the same throughout a descent; automatic pressure sensors and controllers adjust the waste-gate to maintain whatever pressure the pilot has selected. Because the engine doesn't "know" the altitude at which it's operating, there's no concern about adjusting mixture strength during a descent, and it's unlikely that you'll increase the power setting when you level at a lower altitude. If you intend to continue in cruise for an extended period of time at the lower altitude, you should readjust the mixture strength to accommodate the change in air temperature.

Whether you're flying behind an 85 horsepower four-banger or between a pair of 350-horse monsters, full rich is required at the very end of the flight—somewhere on final approach when the power setting is so low that a radical change in mixture strength won't make any difference, and early enough so that you'll have full power instantly available in the event a go-around is required. Believe this: If you open the throttle for a go-around with the mixture in any position except full rich, you will probably get something less than full power, or badly burned valves, or some other kind of engine damage because of over-heating. A quick check of mixture-control position should be the first step in power application during an aborted approach.

Be Careful with the Big Ones

Today's aircraft engines are built with several kinds of metals— iron, nickel, aluminum, steel, and various alloys—with widely varying coefficients of contraction and expansion. Sudden temperature changes are to avoided like the plague, because of the thermal stresses that have a high potential for producing cracks and structural failures.

This is especially true of the big turbocharged engines that operate at very high temperatures and pressures; the rapid descents that are normal in high-altitude operations present a special case for engine cooling precautions. These engines must be treated with kid gloves when it comes to reducing power. Although we're not aware of any official publications in this regard, a sensible cooling schedule has somehow developed in the pilot community, and although it may not be "approvable," we share it with you as a means of taking a reasonable approach to the problem.

Most descents from high altitude (for now, let "high altitude" mean above 10,000 feet) can and should be conducted at cruise power in order to reap the benefits of speed. But sooner or later, you've got to reduce power—if for no other reason than to get the airspeed below the limits for gear and flap extension. When that time comes, it's the kiss of death to pull the throttles back suddenly and significantly; the engine will certainly be damaged—perhaps only a little, but will be damaged nonetheless—by the shock cooling. And if this is done frequently enough, failure may well result.

There's a better way. It requires considerable planning, but you'll be comfortable in knowing that you are taking steps to prevent engine damage from rapid cooling. We suggest that you reduce power in two-inch increments with two-minute cooling periods at each power level.

The planning involves a determination of the power setting required for level flight in the landing pattern (or the initial stage of an instrument approach procedure) and in the configuration you normally use at that stage of a flight. This will be the "bottom line" of your cooling schedule. Divide the difference between the cruise/descent manifold pressure by two (the cooling time periods), and the result will be the number of minutes needed for the cooling process. That's how far out you'll need to begin the cool-down.

The fly in the ointment is non-standard, i.e. other than straight-line descents, in which ATC vectors you around traffic or to an approach gate, or in which you need to deviate for weather or adjust airspeed for turbulent conditions. But experience will improve your ability to take these aberrations into account; the worst that can happen is a bad estimate, and you wind up flying level at a relatively low airspeed because you started the power reduction too soon. Not to worry, that's a small price to pay for damage prevention; just keep thinking of the cost of an early engine overhaul caused by thermal stress cracks.

The concern for engine cool-down shouldn't end with the landing. The turbocharger turbine wheels have been subjected to rather extreme temperatures ever since engine start, and a few minutes at idle power does wonders for them. Make it a habit to leave the throttles at idle as you taxi in—or at least no more power than is needed to move at a reasonable speed—and if that doesn't take two or three minutes, fill out the airplane time sheet or clean up the cockpit before you stop the engines. Do everything you can to slow down temperature changes in those big, expensive power-plants.

A Carburetor Makes a Darn Good Refrigerator

We discussed carburetor icing in an earlier volume of the *Command Decision Series,* but it deserves additional mention in this section on engine performance. If nothing else, keep in mind that whenever carburetor heat is applied, *engine performance will be adversely affected*—whether there's ice present or not.

The introduction of warm air to the carburetor means the introduction of less dense air—fewer air molecules per unit of volume. When carburetor heat is applied to a properly adjusted fuel-air mixture, there will be an instant, noticeable power loss (probably some roughness as well) and the only way to restore smooth engine operation is to lean the mixture. There goes more power—it's inevitable. If you're on a long trip and it appears you'll need carburetor heat the rest of the way, rethink your en route planning. An unscheduled stop may be required.

One of the near-reflexive responses to most inflight engine problems is to move the mixture control to full rich, right now. If carburetor ice is indeed the problem, that's a bad move; the icing itself will have richened the mixture by choking off some of the airflow, and adding more fuel complicates things. Fortunately, carburetor icing doesn't very often jump out of the bushes unannounced; high humidity and visible moisture are red flags, but an alert pilot will notice a slow, steady decrease of power as ice begins to accumulate in the induction system. With a fixed-pitch prop, engine speed will decrease slowly in level flight even though the throttle setting remains unchanged, followed by a decay of airspeed—the latter is the most noticeable warning with a constant-speed propeller.

A little troubleshooting goes a long way here; the application of full carburetor heat to a properly adjusted engine will result in a power decay that would remain constant if there were no ice in the system—the drop in power was due solely to the introduction of hot air. When ice is present, there will be a power decay usually accompanied by roughness as the ice is melted and moved through the engine; after the initial shuddering, power should return to the level you'd expect with carburetor heat alone.

There are three schools of thought with regard to the use of carburetor heat in a known icing environment; one espouses the continued use of full heat to prevent the formation of any more ice, one suggests the use of full heat until the ice is cleared, then wait for indications of icing and go through the routine again, and one recommends a carburetor heat setting that will keep the induction air sufficiently warm to prevent the formation of ice.

The first procedure is an err-on-the-safe-side approach to the problem, but wastes a lot of fuel and power. The second requires the pilot's constant attention and risks getting into considerable trouble if the icing problem is ignored when you're busy with other pilot duties. And the third procedure, although probably the most efficient, should not be attempted without a carburetor-air temperature gauge to insure that the moisture being vaporized by the heat is not cooling and freezing on induction system surfaces farther downstream.

Landing Performance 5

A normal landing is just about whatever a pilot wants it to be. Some prefer full flaps, others like to land routinely with no flaps at all; some like to land with a bit of power, others would rather power down and glide to the ground. There are other landing techniques—some good, some not so good—that vary from one pilot to the next, but as long as there's enough runway to contain the landing roll, well, it's a free country! But consider for a moment the positive aspects of developing a really good landing technique, one that puts your airplane smoothly on the ground in the same configuration and at nearly the same airspeed every time.

First, you—and your passengers—will appreciate the professionalism displayed by a smooth, confident touchdown. It's a lot like boating in that regard; what would you think of a skipper who banged into the dock at the end of every boat ride? No matter how well he handled the rest of the trip, you'll remember the landings—and you may have reservations about his skill when the chips are down. In effect, passengers "grade" pilots on every trip, and the landing is certain to be a critical area. You should be even more critical of yourself.

Second, there's a lot to be said for developing a landing technique that's the same every time so that you can tell when wind, turbulence, airplane weight, or density altitude are working to change an otherwise normal approach. If you don't know what a proper approach looks and feels like, how can you hope to correct for those effects?

Figure 5-1

NORMAL LANDING DISTANCES

ASSOCIATED CONDITIONS

POWER — OFF
FLAPS — 35°
GEAR — DOWN
RUNWAY — PAVED, LEVEL, DRY SURFACE
WEIGHT — 2750 POUNDS
APPROACH SPEED — 85 MPH/74 KTS IAS

NOTES:
1. GROUND ROLL IS APPROXIMATELY 45% OF TOTAL DISTANCE OVER 50 FT. OBSTACLE
2. FOR EACH 100 LBS. BELOW 2750 LBS. REDUCE TABULATED DISTANCE BY 3% AND APPROACH SPEED BY 1 MPH.

WIND COMPONENT DOWN RUNWAY KNOTS	SEA LEVEL OAT °F	TOTAL OVER 50 FT OBSTACLE FEET	2000 FT OAT °F	TOTAL OVER 50 FT OBSTACLE FEET	4000 FT OAT °F	TOTAL OVER 50 FT OBSTACLE FEET	6000 FT OAT °F	TOTAL OVER 50 FT OBSTACLE FEET	8000 FT OAT °F	TOTAL OVER 50 FT OBSTACLE FEET
0	23	1578	16	1651	9	1732	2	1820	-6	1916
	41	1624	34	1701	27	1787	20	1880	13	1983
	59	1670	52	1752	45	1842	38	1942	31	2050
	77	1717	70	1804	63	1899	56	2004	49	2118
	95	1764	88	1856	81	1956	74	2066	66	2187
15	23	1329	16	1397	9	1472	2	1555	-6	1644
	41	1372	34	1444	27	1524	20	1611	13	1707
	59	1414	52	1491	45	1575	38	1668	31	1770
	77	1458	70	1540	63	1626	56	1727	49	1833
	95	1502	88	1588	81	1682	74	1784	66	1898
30	23	1079	16	1142	9	1212	2	1289	-6	1372
	41	1119	34	1186	27	1260	20	1341	13	1430
	59	1158	52	1230	45	1308	38	1395	31	1489
	77	1199	70	1275	63	1357	56	1449	49	1548
	95	1240	88	1320	81	1407	74	1502	66	1608

In the third place, safety is enhanced by "grooving" an approach and landing technique that uses something less than the entire runway; the ability to get good *normal* landing performance from your airplane is a good foundation for carrying off a *maximum-performance* effort when it's required.

The Charts Tell the Story

Consider Figures 5-1 and 5-2, which are typical landing performance presentations; one in tabular form, the other a graph. The conditions obviously include corrections for density altitude, airplane weight and wind, and you are probably not surprised to discover that there are no power considerations—with the engine at idle, normal landing performance is based on an aerodynamic body gliding through the air. This is one exercise that requires a great deal of pilot technique to make the numbers work.

The laws of physics dominate, tempered somewhat by the condition of the wheel brakes and how hard the pilot is willing to press on the pedals. If the airplane touches the ground at a certain speed, a certain amount of energy must be exchanged to get it stopped in the published distance; in this case, the energy of motion is changed to heat energy, generated by the friction of braking. The attainment of these landing performance numbers is therefore very dependent on accurate touchdown speeds; quite simply, the faster you're moving at ground contact, the longer the landing distance. And that will be a *lot* longer for really "hot" landings. Good airspeed control is very important, and is a worthwhile objective in your quest for consistently good landings.

Notice that both of these charts call for a specific airspeed at a specific altitude (50 feet above the runway), and a power-off, full-flap descent from that point to the surface. It would take a genuine wizard to achieve all of that every time in a glide, so the more likely technique is to fly a partially powered approach at the prescribed airspeed until reaching the 50-foot point, then power down for landing.

The point here is not that test-pilot accuracy may be required to achieve book figures; rather, pilots need to be aware of the consequences when any one of the several factors involved gets outside reasonable limits. For example, landing distance will be remarkably increased if the airspeed is 10 knots too high, or if the

Figure 5-2

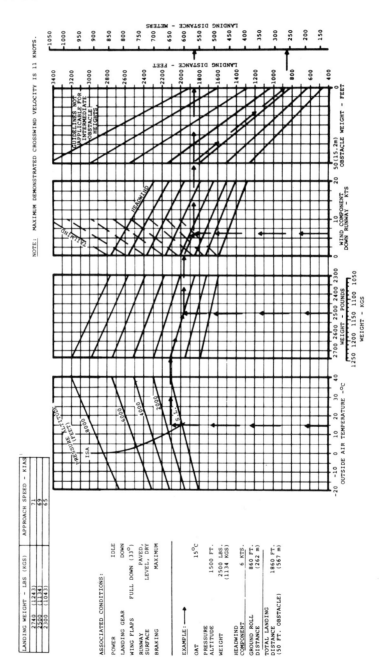

NORMAL LANDING DISTANCE

wing flaps aren't fully extended, or if there's a tailwind; the list goes on and on. It doesn't take much of a distraction to let one of these factors get out of hand and cause trouble.

The weather was generally good VFR at Billings, Montana. There was a layer of broken clouds at 5,000 feet, visibility 10 miles in light rain showers, and the wind was blowing from 220 degrees at 10 knots. A Comanche pilot had been struggling a bit to maintain VFR on his way to Billings, and the rain showers kept him from sighting the airport until he was almost directly overhead.

The approach controller advised the pilot to plan his landing on Runway 9R, a suggestion that should have been carefully evaluated, because it would require landing downwind on a 3,800-foot runway. When the Comanche was handed off to the tower, the airplane was directly over the airport, and the local controller was concerned about the pilot's ability to get down on Runway 9; "Would you like to have Runway 4?" he asked. "Yeah," said the pilot, "I can try that."

As the Comanche maneuvered, it appeared that the pilot was confused, and the controller radioed "You're on the wrong runway there, go around." Six seconds later, he reconsidered and said "Okay, if you can make Runway 4 from that point, that's fine. If not, just keep circling and make left traffic for that runway."

If the pilot wasn't confused initially, he certainly might have been after those transmissions, but he tried to land on Runway 4 anyway. Witnesses indicated that the Comanche touched down almost two-thirds of the way down the runway. Skid marks began approximately 1,000 feet from the end, and tracked the runway centerline until about the last 300 feet, when the airplane began to drift to the right. The Comanche then skidded off the runway and continued for 100 feet through a grassy overrun where the nose landing gear was sheared off.

At this point, the ground drops off abruptly and the airplane, now airborne again, sailed another 130 feet before striking the ground in a near-vertical attitude. The pilot was killed by the impact, the passenger seriously injured.

Weather was undoubtedly a factor in this accident. Even though the pilot was instrument rated, he made no effort to "go IFR" when he encountered rain and clouds during his approach to Billings. He told the tower controller at one point, "It looks like if I continue on this heading, I'm going to go IFR," which may have been preferable to the hurry-up, high-speed, everything-happens-at-the-last-minute approach that took place.

The tailwind certainly played a part. An airline captain who landed on Runway 9 shortly before the accident saw the Comanche go by, but thought the pilot was taking off—the airspeed and altitude were higher than normal. The airliner had problems with the tailwind as well; the maximum tailwind component for the Boeing 727 is 10 knots, and in the captain's words, "We really had to honk on the brakes to get the airplane stopped in the runway remaining."

Post-accident investigation of the wreckage showed that the Comanche's wing flaps were extended only nine degrees (one notch), a setting recommended for short-field takeoffs, but inadequate for a normal landing. A downwind approach, too much airspeed, too little flaps and not enough runway added up to disaster for this pilot. When in doubt, go around.

Not Too Much, Not Too Little, But Just Right

Airspeed is the key to successful landings. Those who err on the low side may perform "controlled crashes" or "arrivals" more than landings, because when the airplane quits flying several feet above the runway, there's seldom time to recover before ground contact.

There are also problems for the pilot who figures that if some is good, more is better. The "five knots for the wife and kids" philosophy has been the undoing of a lot of aviators. Concern for stalling close to the ground is probably high on the list of apprehensions for most pilots, but flying approaches at a higher, ostensibly safer airspeed creates more hazard than it prevents.

As we've seen, extra airspeed means additional distance because of the sheer energy involved, but there are aerodynamic considerations as well. Down close to the runway, ground effect

Airspeed is the critical key to successful landings. This is especially true in high-performance singles like the Bonanza.

comes into play and effectively increases airspeed as the wings develop more lift; the airplane just won't flare because every time the pilot eases back on the control wheel to round out, there's enough lift to make the airplane climb. This is usually followed by a bit of forward pressure, whereupon the airplane descends back into the heart of ground effect and the process repeats itself.

At this point—especially if the end of the runway is closing fast—some pilots will attempt to force the airplane onto the ground with forward pressure on the wheel. And it works—but in order to stay on the ground, more forward pressure is required and in extreme cases, there is enough aerodynamic lift at this excessive speed to raise the main wheels off the runway. Instead of an airplane, the pilot is now in command of a wheelbarrow with wings, a vehicle that's very difficult to steer. The only solution is an immediate go-around; that *has* to be done properly if the day is to be saved.

A student pilot suffered minor injuries when his Cessna 152 bounced and went out of control during a downwind

Figure 5-3

OBSTACLE LANDING DISTANCES

ASSOCIATED CONDITIONS

POWER — AS REQUIRED TO MAINTAIN 800 FT/MIN ON FINAL APPROACH
FLAPS — 35°
GEAR — DOWN
RUNWAY — PAVED, LEVEL, DRY SURFACE
WEIGHT — 2750 LBS.
APPROACH — 76 MPH/66 KTS IAS

NOTES:

1. GROUND ROLL IS APPROXIMATELY 55% OF TOTAL DISTANCE OVER 50 FT. OBSTACLE
2. FOR EACH 100 POUNDS BELOW 2750 LBS, REDUCE TABULATED DISTANCE BY 3% AND APPROACH SPEED BY 1 MPH.

WIND COMPONENT DOWN RUNWAY KNOTS	SEA LEVEL OAT °F	SEA LEVEL TOTAL OVER 50 FT OBSTACLE FEET	2000 FT OAT °F	2000 FT TOTAL OVER 50 FT OBSTACLE FEET	4000 FT OAT °F	4000 FT TOTAL OVER 50 FT OBSTACLE FEET	6000 FT OAT °F	6000 FT TOTAL OVER 50 FT OBSTACLE FEET	8000 FT OAT °F	8000 FT TOTAL OVER 50 FT OBSTACLE FEET
0	23	1306	16	1365	9	1430	2	1501	-6	1579
	41	1343	34	1405	27	1474	20	1550	13	1633
	59	1380	52	1446	45	1519	38	1599	31	1688
	77	1418	70	1488	63	1565	56	1650	49	1743
	95	1456	88	1530	81	1611	74	1700	66	1799
15	23	1084	16	1139	9	1199	2	1265	-6	1337
	41	1118	34	1176	27	1240	20	1311	13	1388
	59	1153	52	1214	45	1282	38	1356	31	1439
	77	1189	70	1253	63	1324	56	1403	49	1490
	95	1223	88	1292	81	1367	74	1450	66	1542
30	23	861	16	912	9	968	2	1029	-6	1095
	41	893	34	946	27	1005	20	1071	13	1142
	59	925	52	981	45	1044	38	1113	31	1189
	77	957	70	1017	63	1083	56	1156	49	1236
	95	990	88	1053	81	1123	74	1199	66	1284

WARNING: Obstacle take off is not a recommended procedure, as it utilizes speeds at or below power-off stall speed. In the event of engine failure or wind speed fluctuations, a stall may occur which may cause uncontrolled contact with the ground.

landing at the end of a solo cross-country flight. He attempted a full-flap landing on Runway 17, but the plane bounced and departed the runway to the left. The pilot added full power and tried to go around, but left the flaps fully extended. The aircraft did not accelerate to flying speed and struck a fence and a tree off the runway.

The 3,445-foot paved runway is at an elevation of 4,333 feet MSL, a factor that had a negative effect on the 152's performance, but the wind was the big problem. The pilot said although he thought the wind had been from the south, he later discovered that it was from 010 degrees at 15 knots, gusting to 20; he didn't use Unicom to determine the wind conditions, even though he knew it was available.

The pilot also told investigators that he saw no wind sock, and although he observed the traffic direction indicator, he misread it by 180 degrees because he had never seen one before.

Maximum Performance Landings: Short- and Soft-Field Procedures

The landing distances published in the Pilot's Operating Handbook are another figment of test pilot and aeronautical engineer data manipulation. Sure, the good book says that by taking into account the pressure altitude, outside air temperature, wind, and aircraft weight, you should be able to clear a 50-foot obstacle, touch down, and come to a stop in x number of feet. Maybe so, but what airspeed and power setting and glide angle on the final approach produce that kind of performance? What does "maximum braking" mean? Have you ever practiced this kind of short-field approach and roll-out? The test pilot has! And the engineer has discarded any data that resulted from poor technique, lack of practice, or negative effects of atmospheric turbulence; he waited for his pilot to come up with good, consistent figures on just the right kind of day. And don't forget that the test pilot is doing his work on a long, wide runway with only imaginary obstacles—none of the "real stuff" you may encounter in actual operating conditions (Figure 5-3 and 5-4).

A genuine short-field approach and landing—that is, achieving something close to the handbook values—may exceed reasonable limitations for the average pilot, unless he is well taught and gets

Figure 5-4

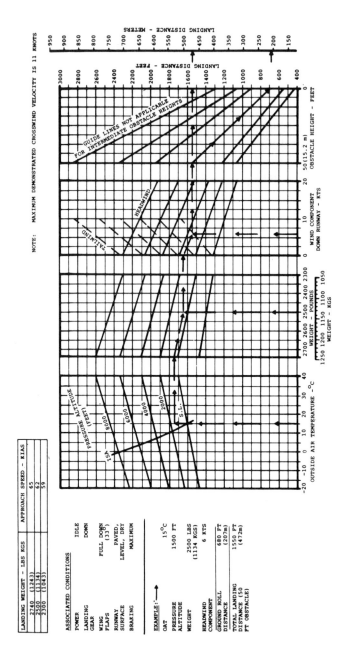

MAXIMUM PERFORMANCE LANDING DISTANCE

a lot of practice. Even then, squeezing maximum performance out of any airplane is an exercise fraught with hazard, because you're operating at the very edge of the airplane's capabilities, and doing it very close to the ground. The requirement to cross the 50-foot point at a very low airspeed with the throttle closed, and in a full-flap, high-drag configuration makes this operation very much like autorotation practice in a helicopter: you've got to get it right the first time.

In an airplane with really effective wing flaps, the "barn doors" that generate large amounts of drag, the situation can get even touchier. The ubiquitous Cessna 150 series, for example, can produce an idle-power descent at 30 to 40 percent above stall speed that looks like a Kamikaze dive to an outside observer. There is barely enough energy left at the bottom to complete a landing flare and touchdown before stalling. Don't try this maneuver without a lot of practice at a safe altitude, and even then, we suggest that you add 25 to 50 percent to the handbook values for landing over an obstacle.

And how about "maximum braking?" It's been defined as "an 80 percent rolling skid," a condition in which the tire is rolling at a speed slightly slower than the airplane's groundspeed, leaving a lot of rubber on the runway, but producing the most friction. That's a rather subjective determination, especially when you're rapidly running out of runway. The proper amount of brake pressure can be achieved only after much practice and experimentation; don't count on "maximum braking" the first time you really need it.

In summary, a maximum-performance landing is a high-proficiency operation, and it's unlikely that you'll be able to get an airplane stopped in the distance published in the POH. There are just too many variables, too many factors working against you. Considering that there are few airplanes capable of taking off in the same distance required for landing, the importance of risking all to get into a field you probably can't get out of begins to pale.

When it comes to maximum-performance landings, conservatism is a virtue.

Multi-Engine Performance

Throughout these sections dealing with aircraft performance, we have given short shrift to the pluses—and problems—of operating a twin-engine airplane, and with good reason. In the first place, multi-engine performance is rather unique in several respects, not the least of which is airplane behavior following an engine failure; secondly, we wanted to put all of this information in one place for your convenience; not all of you are interested in multi-engine performance. The nature of the beast provides two obvious categories for discussion; performance considerations with both engines running, and with one shut down. We'll take a look at performance with *no* engines running in the next section.

There are significant differences in the certification rules for "large" airplanes—those with maximum takeoff weights above 12,500 pounds—and those that fall into the "transport aircraft" category. In general, these multi-engine airplanes must have enough power remaining in the operating engine so that the takeoff and climb can be continued if an engine fails on the runway; some of the smaller twins can, some can't. We'll explore both sets of circumstances.

Takeoff and Climb Performance:
Both Engines Operating

Light twins sound and look faster than their single-engine kin, and for the most part, they are faster; but don't expect huge increases in climb rates and overall takeoff performance just because there are two powerplants; the additional power supplied by another engine falls well short of doubling the performance. Turboprops and turbojets are another story, because the extra power is provided with relatively little additional weight. That means more power per pound, and accounts for the tremendous increase in climb rates, cruise altitudes and airspeeds for jet-powered airplanes.

The takeoff performance of a light twin depends on weight, wind, and density altitude just like other airplanes—the laws of physics have no respect for the number of powerplants installed. But there's one factor that provides a limitation for every multi-engine takeoff; it's Vmc, the velocity for minimum control, and it provides an airspeed baseline for all takeoff calculations and techniques. A quick review is in order.

When one of the engines fails in flight, the airplane will experience an immediate and significant yaw toward the dead engine. The pilot is expected to use rudder and aileron pressure as required to return the airplane to straight flight and maintain that condition, but it can only be done within the limits of flight control authority. In other words, there's an airspeed below which the rudder/aileron combination hasn't enough airflow to work with to offset the asymmetrical thrust when this minimum airspeed is reached, the airplane *will* yaw and roll toward the dead engine.

With that in mind, no multi-engine pilot in his right mind would permit his airplane to leave the ground until Vmc has been attained; even though the airplane is capable of lift-off at a much lower speed (as all twins are), it's sheer folly to fly unless the airspeed indicator is beyond the magic number. That eliminates the possibility of losing control should an engine quit between lift-off and the attainment of Vmc—a situation that would certainly be a disaster that close to the ground. Most normal takeoff-distance charts or tables specify a lift-off speed five knots or so above Vmc; that's also the criteria used for evaluating applicants for multi-engine ratings. A little cushion in the interest of safety.

Right from the start of his takeoff planning, the pilot of a recip twin must think in terms of options. Whereas the pilot of a single-engine plane has only one thing to do in the event of engine failure during the takeoff roll, the multi-engine pilot might be able to (1) come to a safe stop on the remaining runway or (2) continue the takeoff. Because both of these options involve problems encoun-

Figure 6-1

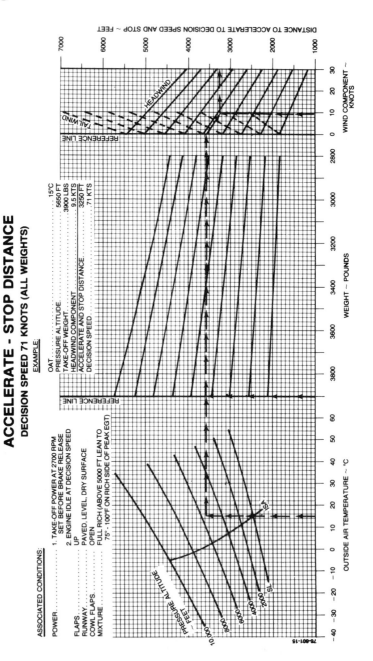

tered during the period when airspeed is building up toward the lift-off value, they have been labeled "accelerate-stop" and "accelerate-go." (See Figure 6-1.)

Option Number 1 can be quantified by applying the takeoff factors—wind, weight, density altitude—to the stopping power of the airplane's brakes at a given velocity. An example is a typical Accelerate-Stop Distance table for a light twin; all the factors are there, plus a "decision speed" (Vmc plus a safety cushion), and the result is the number of feet required to start the takeoff roll, accelerate to the published decision speed, suffer the loss of one engine, and brake to a stop. If the accelerate-stop distance is greater than the length of the runway, don't go—defuel, unload some passengers, wait for a lower density altitude, but don't go in this condition. (The "decision speed" in this example is a convenient number which adequately covers the weight range of this airplane. With a larger airplane, and a wider range of takeoff weights, the manufacturer will provide appropriate decision speeds throughout the range.)

The accelerate-go chart (Figure 6-2) looks nearly identical because it uses the same factors, but the result is quite different. This chart provides the distance required from brake release to 50 feet above the runway *with an engine failure at lift-off*. For a given set of conditions, the accelerate-go distance will always be a lot greater than accelerate-stop.

So, the multi-engine pilot must consider at least three limitations when making the go/no-go decision; is there enough runway for a normal takeoff, for accelerate-stop, and for accelerate-go? If any one of these distances exceeds runway length, don't go; disregard for these values violates common sense *and* the regulation that prohibits operation of an aircraft beyond its operational limitations. (Accelerate-go distance may be tempered somewhat by conditions that exist beyond the end of the runway, i.e. level, unbroken terrain might provide a satisfactory environment for continuing the climb. But don't fail to consider the notoriously poor climb gradient of most light twins. You might not be able to get over or around every obstacle in your path. It makes a lot more sense to accept runway length as the limit for accelerate-go.)

Figure 6-2

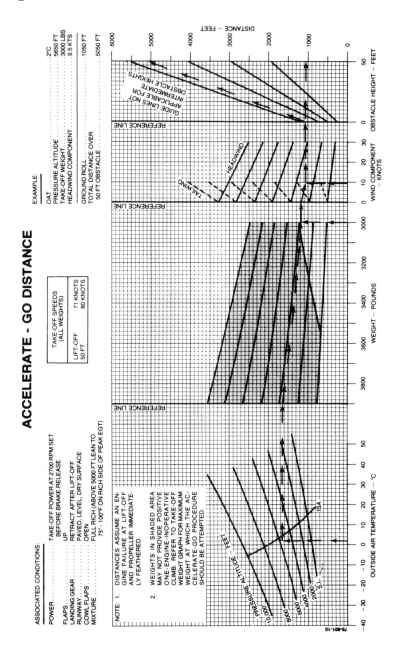

Climbing with an Engine Out

The loss of half of the power output of a light twin cuts a lot deeper when you consider the loss of climb performance. The high-drag configuration that results as a pilot attempts to maintain straight flight robs an enormous amount of climb capability; on the order of 80 percent. For example, if your light twin climbs at 1000 feet per minute with both engines running at full power, expect no more than 200 fpm when one of them quits. Sure, that's a positive number, but consider the flat climb gradient; at a groundspeed of 120 knots (2 miles per minute), you're climbing at only 100 feet per mile. That would provide an up-close tour of a lot of real estate off the end of the runway.

One way to get around the specter of low-performance climb (which is characteristic of the light-twin population; nothing wrong with the airplanes, that's the best they can do with the power that remains following an engine failure) is to lighten the load before takeoff. There's statistical evidence that fatal light-twin accidents are related to power loading—the number of pounds per installed horsepower. The break point seems to be at or near a value of 10 pounds per horsepower, with the airplanes loaded above that number being more likely to cause fatalities. An airplane with a high power loading just won't climb very much, and if the pilot tries to force the issue, airspeed drops off, Vmc rears its very ugly head, and the resultant out-of-control crash really hurts people.

Once again, weight is the most important factor, and it's completely under the control of the pilot. You might consider never attempting a takeoff unless you have reduced the gross weight so as to bring the power loading value below 10 (somewhat limiting when it comes to useful load, but mighty comforting when one of the engines blows its stack right after takeoff).

Single-engine rate-of-climb graphs or charts present a rather fuzzy picture. If you review a library of POHs for typical piston twins and check their single-engine climb rates, you'll find that they are remarkably similar. Then check the rate of climb on one engine versus the stall speed, and sure enough, the planes with the higher stall speeds have the higher single-engine climb rates. Why? Because the certification requirements tie climb rate to stall speed, and the manufacturers generally go for the highest gross weight that will allow them to pass the single-engine climb rate for their stall speed at that weight. Thus, most twins fall into the 200- to 300-fpm single-engine rate of climb category. The turboprops come out better, because many of them are essentially recip-engined airplanes fitted with more powerful turboprops, but without sufficient structural beef-up to allow a significant gross weight increase.

The variable part of the average light or medium weight twin single-engine climb performance is the test pilot/weather/winds/turbulence factor again. The test pilot only gathers his data on clear, calm days. If one of *your* two engines should fail at night, in IMC, and close to the ground, don't count on getting handbook performance on the remaining engine. Don't count on any more than *half* of the published single-engine rate of climb figure. You are experiencing an emergency, you don't have a good visual horizon, you are not already trimmed for Vyse like the test pilot was, and you have other problems, like shutting down the offending engine. The test pilot already knew which engine would be failed, and he has it secured before even starting his climb test. Also, the test pilot assumes a *complete* engine failure—he doesn't fool around with a possible "partial-power-on-the-bad-engine" scenario—he just feathers the propeller on the engine that was programmed to fail. If he runs into rough air that would render the data meaningless, he just quits the test and tries again the next day.

Fatal Indecision

Pilots pay a high price for the extra performance and systems redundancy provided by piston-powered twins. The payment we're concerned with here is not in the form of hard dollars, it's a levy imposed by the possibility of an engine failure at the worst possible time—on takeoff.

In this situation, there must be an investment in skill and judgment if the pilot hopes to maintain control and exploit the meager performance that's still available to bring the flight to a safe conclusion.

Records show that one in every 10 accidents involving piston twins occurs when pilots are unable to pay the price. There's no doubt that an engine failure on takeoff is one of aviation's toughest challenges. Loss of control is the penalty for any delay in response or flaw in pilot technique.

Those who would assume that such mishaps befall only the inexperienced will be surprised to learn that they typically involve pilots with thousands of hours of flying experience and hundreds of hours in type.

Furthermore, accident reports often reveal that pilots react improperly—or not at all—to engine failures in piston twins. In many cases, airspeed is permitted to decay until control is lost and the airplane rolls inverted. Landing gear and flaps are left extended. The propeller on the dead engine is left windmilling. In haste or confusion the wrong engine is shut down.

Such an accident occurred several years ago, and the results of the investigation provide a few clues about why experienced multi-engine pilots sometimes do not respond successfully to the challenge of an engine failure on takeoff.

The airplane, a Piper Chieftain, was a commuter airline workhorse. The pilots were ATPs, with plenty of aviation experience. The captain had done a lot of multi-engine instruction before joining the airline; nearly a third of his 4,300 hours of flight time were in piston twins. His experience included more than 800 hours in Chieftains.

In the right seat was a new-hire who was being groomed to become a captain for the commuter airline. The "captain trainee" was along on this flight just to observe, learn the routes, and help the captain with the baggage; he had been assigned no copilot duties. A former instructor and examiner in Air Force C-141s, the pilot had flown most of his 3,250 hours in multi-engine jets; he had no previous experience in light piston twins.

Delays during the three trips the crew already had flown had put them well behind schedule when the Chieftain landed at Houston's Hobby Airport shortly after 7 p.m. The airplane was late for its scheduled departure to Brownsville, Texas. The weather was clear and the temperature was 56 degrees F.

Perhaps hurrying to make up some time, the captain used his company's approved average passenger weight figures in preparing the load manifest. His calculations

Although it has 700 horsepower, Piper's Chieftain has a relatively poor single-engine climb rate.

indicated that with two pilots, eight passengers and baggage, the Chieftain would be right at its maximum gross weight of 7,000 pounds and at its aft CG limit of 135 inches. Unfortunately, several of the occupants obviously weighed much more than the FAA-approved averages; four of the passengers—and the captain, himself—weighed more than 200 pounds apiece.

According to calculations by the NTSB investigators, the Chieftain was actually 280 pounds over max gross weight and the CG was 3 inches behind the aft limit. However, the Board determined that the extra weight would not have affected the Chieftain's single-engine performance to any great extent, noting that the tendency of the airplane to yaw into the failed engine would have been more pronounced than normal because of the aft CG. The captain would have needed to apply more rudder pressure than normal during such an emergency to counteract the yaw.

Thirty minutes after landing in Houston, the Chieftain taxied out for takeoff, was promptly cleared into position on Runway 22, and after waiting a couple of minutes on the runway, was cleared to take off.

> Another pilot, waiting to depart on Runway 22 at the same time, recalled that the Chieftain had not used the run-up area, and it appeared that the crew never performed a pre-takeoff check of the Chieftain's engines. The tower controller noticed the Chieftain begin a bank at about 100 feet, and asked the crew if they would be making a right turn away from the airport. The response, by the captain-in-training, was, "We just lost the right engine."

According to the NTSB reconstruction of the takeoff, the Chieftain was 90 feet above the runway when the right engine lost power. The landing gear had been retracted, but the flaps were still at the 15-degree takeoff setting. Indicated airspeed was at or just below 109 knots, the published best single-engine rate of climb speed (Vyse). At that speed, the airplane had a 30-knot buffer above its minimum single-engine control speed (Vmc).

The emergency procedures section of the Chieftain flight manual provides two options for a pilot who experiences a power loss on takeoff: "If engine failure occurs when sufficient airspeed above Vmc is obtained, the pilot must decide whether to abort the takeoff or attempt a single-engine takeoff. His decision should be based on his judgment, considering the runway remaining, density altitude, loading, obstructions, weather and his own capability."

In this case, the NTSB was of the opinion that aborting the takeoff and landing straight ahead would have been the better option. There was plenty of room to do so; Runway 22 is 7,600 feet long and has a flat 1,300-foot clear zone off the end that is obstructed only by approach lights. The Board said that if the crew had reduced power on the left engine, lowered the gear and extended full flaps, they probably could have brought the Chieftain to a stop with minimum damage. They would have used up all of the remaining runway and about half of the clear zone.

> After the captain-trainee reported the engine failure, the Chieftain maintained runway heading for about 10 seconds before beginning a right turn and a shallow descent.

The turn and descent rate steepened, and the wings were leveled just before the airplane crashed on a parking ramp 90 degrees off the runway heading. It slid into two other planes, four vehicles and a hangar.

Three passengers survived with serious injuries; the other five occupants were killed.

The NTSB concluded that the engine failure at a critical moment during the takeoff and the Chieftain's "marginal" single-engine performance capability were probable causes of the crash. The cause of the engine failure was never determined because of extensive fire damage.

The Board also faulted the captain's incorrect response to the emergency—that is, his failure to either land on the remaining runway or configure the airplane to sustain single-engine flight. The Chieftain crashed with its flaps still extended 15 degrees, and the *left* propeller had been feathered—the right one had failed.

Considering the captain's extensive experience as a multi-engine instructor, he should have been able to handle this emergency. The NTSB proposed one possible explanation for his failure to do so: "Apparently, the captain was not mentally prepared to analyze and respond to the engine failure."

Beyond this rather tentative conclusion, the investigation revealed very little about the human factors aspects of this accident. There was no examination of the captain's physical and mental state. Nor did the Board look into any possible interactions between the captain and the "captain-in-training."

Someday, human factors research may provide us with a clearer understanding of why such mistakes are made repeatedly by otherwise well-trained and experienced pilots. In the meantime, we suspect that what the NTSB postulated about the Chieftain captain's lack of mental preparation may be a prominent factor in this type of mishap.

It's not just the complacency that tends to take root in a pilot's psyche after dozens, perhaps hundreds of uneventful takeoffs, or the comforting defense mechanism that lulls a pilot into thinking that engine failures are rare and happen only to "other pilots." We suspect that also involved here is the inability of even the best initial and recurrent multi-engine training to prepare a pilot to react *instinctively* to an engine failure on takeoff.

There are tough choices to make, complex procedures to follow and very little time in which to act.

Mental preparation is the key. An engine failure has to be expected and planned for; emergency procedures that must be performed from memory must be mentally rehearsed.

Then, and only then, can a pilot be confident that he is ready to meet the challenge of takeoff in a multi-engine airplane.

Emergency Performance

Silence is golden, except in an airplane, where a sudden lack of noise means trouble—usually *big* trouble. There was a time when aircraft engines were so unreliable that pilots were surprised if they got through an entire flight without a failure. Today, we have grown very complacent because modern powerplants run for long periods of time without missing a beat, and that complacency sets us up for something less than a timely, correct reaction when an engine actually quits in flight.

Obviously, aircraft performance undergoes major reductions when an engine fails. The single-engine pilot must make immediate plans for a forced landing; the multi-engine pilot should also plan to land soon, but the ability to remain in the air takes most of the immediacy out of his decision.

Good training, continued frequent practice, and constant in-flight awareness of the situation with regard to "what would I do if an engine failure occurred right now?" are the key issues in handling an emergency like this. There are ways to milk the maximum performance out of an airplane that's powerless or nearly so, and that's what we'll discuss in this section.

Is It Really All Gone?

A good flight training program stresses the importance of quick response to power failures, and will develop that skill in a student through repeated practice—a simulated engine-out on just about every takeoff in the early stages of training, and more simulations at times when the instructor figures his student least expects an engine problem. Repeated drills are at the heart of good emergency procedure training; take care of the critical items right now and in the proper order—there may be time to trouble-shoot and perhaps undo the emergency after the situation is well in hand. Particularly with regard to single-engine aircraft, it's much better to assume that a significant change in the sound of the powerplant or its indicators is the prelude to a complete power loss. The pilot who goes through the engine-failure procedure has a leg up if the failure turns out to be only a partial one.

For the single-engine flier, some power is always better than none, because any thrust can be used to increase the "hang time," if you will, and perhaps let you reach a more accommodating forced-landing site. If nothing else, that extra time provides an opportunity to fly a better engine-out pattern, to get better prepared for a crash landing, to re-order your mental state, and time to do a better job overall. Don't worry about ruining an engine that's running rough, or backfiring; whatever the damage, it's already done, and even if you should turn it into junk on the way to an airport or a better landing spot, the price of another engine is minuscule compared to the price of a disaster. The only exceptions to this philosophy should be an engine fire, or vibration so strong you have concerns about the engine shaking itself off the mounts.

The multi-engine pilot has more options, although they are largely overlooked in training; very few instructors simulate partial-power configurations. In the more likely situation, students are trained to react to any interruption in engine output like Pavlov's dog: "Fly the airplane, identify the failed engine, feather the offending propeller..." No concern for determining whether the "failed" engine might be putting out enough power to carry its weight. Even the emergency procedures in the Pilot's Operating Handbooks assume complete engine failure, and that's not always the case.

Once again, some power is better than none, and with a multi-engine airplane, it's even better than that; any power greater than zero thrust will keep Vmc at arm's length, and that's a good deal. Here's what can happen when a pilot doesn't recognize a partial-power situation.

A Piper Navajo was scheduled to depart the Greater Cincinnati (Ohio) Airport on a commuter flight with a pilot and seven passengers. It was operating behind schedule because of delays in the first flights of the day, and the

*Multi-engine training stresses—some say overstresses—the impor-
tance of securing a failed engine, but in many cases the engine may be
producing useful power and securing may make matters worse.*

captain was probably hurrying to make up for lost time.

At any rate, the airplane was cleared for takeoff on
Runway 18. An airline captain right behind the commuter
flight said the Navajo turned left onto the runway and
immediately started its takeoff roll.

Post-accident investigation would show that the Piper was loaded
161 pounds above its maximum allowable takeoff weight, with the
CG located 3/4 inch behind the aft limit. The landing gear was down
and locked, the wing flaps were extended 26 degrees—11 degrees
more than the POH recommended for normal takeoff.

The takeoff appeared normal up to the instant of lift-off,
which occurred 1,500-2,000 feet from the start of the
takeoff roll. The pilot "jerked his aircraft into the air," said
the airline captain, "and it began to yaw to the right and
then leveled off 6 to 10 feet above the runway for two to four
seconds before beginning a slow climb. The aircraft yawed

right and left 10 to 20 degrees, and the wings rocked from side to side during the slow climb." The landing gear and wing flaps remained extended. The Navajo pilot reported an engine problem just after lift-off:

Pilot: 444 has just lost an engine, like to come back around.

Tower: Okay, anything you like...you want to make a left turn out and go in on 27?...or whatever you like. You're cleared to land; wind check, one niner at eight. And 444, you want the equipment standing by?

Pilot: Stand by.

The airline captain, his eyes now riveted to the scene, said "the left engine appeared normal, but I could see intermittent flashes of the right propeller as if it were slowed to near-idle rpm."

Another airline pilot said that the Piper never appeared to accelerate and remained in a relatively flat attitude 5 to 10 degrees nose-up. He last saw the airplane rolling and yawing about 150 feet above the center of the runway.

The commuter's Director of Maintenance, standing on a parking ramp east of the runway, said that abnormal engine sounds drew his attention to the aircraft when it was about 150 feet in the air. "It was pulsating...sounded at times to be at high rpm and then cut out...sounded like aircraft wasn't developing full power on the good engine." He also said the aircraft began to descend slightly while in slow flight, with landing gear and flaps extended and the wings rocking back and forth.

Seconds later, the Navajo rolled to the right to an inverted position and dove nose first into the ground. All occupants died in the crash.

The subsequent in-depth investigation and the NTSB review of the accident produced a number of contributing causes; they included the pilot's inexperience in multi-engine airplanes in general and the Navajo in particular, a hurried departure, inadequate training, inexperienced company management, and ineffective FAA certification and surveillance of the operator.

But the probable cause, according to the NTSB, was "the loss of control following a *partial loss of power* (our emphasis) immediate-

ly after liftoff. The Board opined that the accident could have been
avoided if the pilot had either rejected the takeoff or had retracted
the landing gear and wing flaps. His failure to take decisive action
may have been due to preoccupation with correcting the [engine]
malfunction, and a lack of familiarity with the aircraft and its
emergency procedures."

With 7,000 feet or so of runway remaining, this pilot would have
done well to pull back both throttles and land when he sensed a
problem with the right engine. But his attempt to continue the
takeoff illustrates the point that multi-engine training may be a
little over-insistent on that Pavlovian shut-it-down response.

Is Anything Happening Out There?

The trick, of course, is to figure out whether an engine is producing
some power or none at all. The single-engine operator behind a
fixed-pitch propeller has the hardest job of all. The only reliable
indication of partial power is the airplane's glide performance,
which can be compared in terms of a lower-than-normal rate of
descent, or higher-than-normal rpm at the normal glide speed.
Both of these comparisons require knowledge of the normal values.

We emphasize that any such experimentation, particularly in a
single-engine airplane, take place *only* after the airplane has been
set up in the maximum glide configuration and the "Engine Failure
in Flight" checklist has been accomplished. When you suddenly
become a glider pilot, time is of the essence and you shouldn't do
anything that doesn't contribute in a positive way to the safest
possible forced landing; that includes making radio calls.

While you're playing test pilot (something we advocate once in
a while—it helps sharpen your flying skills), find out the minimum
power required to maintain altitude in your airplane. You will
probably be surprised to find that a very low power setting—
perhaps only 25 or 30 percent, maybe less in some cases—is
required to keep things going. True, you'll also be flying at a very
low airspeed, but when you're limping toward safety with a sick
engine, who cares about speed?

A Grumman American AA-5 crashed two miles southwest
of the Municipal Airport in Corona, California, following a
complete power loss shortly after takeoff. Post-accident
investigation disclosed that the dowel pin which secures
the timing gear to the crankshaft had sheared; this malfunction stopped all valve action and ignition timing, very

The Grumman pilot, having suffered an engine failure, delayed his decision to return to the airport. The occupants of the airplane were seriously injured in the resultant off-airport landing.

effectively stopping the engine cold. There was no way the pilot could have restored power.

In his statement, the pilot indicated that the engine quit abruptly at 600 to 700 feet AGL in the climb. There was no backfire, no missing; the engine acted as if it had been "turned off."

Here's where the timing and sequence of a pilot's emergency actions can become critical. Immediately after the engine stopped, this pilot made several Mayday calls, conversed briefly with a helicopter pilot who happened to be on the Unicom frequency, then tried to restart the engine, then began a "slow turn to the south." By this time, so much altitude had been lost that the only landing site was a freshly graded area around a construction site. It might have gone well, but a set of telephone lines interfered, the Tiger crashed and both occupants were seriously injured.

This accident might—we emphasize might—have been prevented or made less damaging if the time spent on the radio had been used to maneuver the airplane to a more hospitable landing site. With plenty of altitude (that's a very subjective determination) and plenty of time, a radio call may be justified, but not if it takes anything away from airspeed control or maneuvering to land.

The same admonition applies to attempts to figure out whether there's any power left in the engine. When you've plenty of altitude (a very subjective determination) and therefore plenty of time to experiment, ease the nose up a degree or two and see if the airplane will do better—you may be operating with partial power, and that may extend your time in the air enough to get you home, or at least to a better place to land.

The multi-engine pilot's choices are not quite so limited when he's faced with an engine failure. Given the severely limited engine-out climb performance of light twins (especially at near-maximum weight), the engine-failure drill should be accomplished in a timely manner; but the procedure itself provides a check on engine performance and the possibility of some power being produced. It makes good sense to check the power output of the affected engine, and here's a positive way to accomplish it.

At some point in the engine-out drill, the throttle of the suspected engine should be moved slowly to the idle position for the express purpose of identifying the dead engine (it gets mighty quiet when a pilot hurries through the shutdown process and feathers the wrong propeller!). At that point in the procedure, the pilot should be maintaining straight flight with whatever rudder and aileron pressure is required, and any change in power output on either side of the airplane will result in an uncommanded yaw.

The expected response to this throttle movement is of course no change at all, indicating that the pilot has positively identified the dead engine, the prop is windmilling, and that there is absolutely no power production. But what if there's a yaw—even a slight amount—toward the dead engine as the throttle is moved back? That could only mean that the engine is putting out some thrust, which the pilot reduced by throttling back. Now, it would be wise to return the throttle to full open and take advantage of the more-than-zero-thrust condition—even if it's only until you can gain enough altitude to feel comfortable with a complete shutdown.

Caution—a relaxation of control pressure because of distraction or improper sensing of yaw could defeat this procedure in a dangerous way. The key to this method is absolute discipline in the heading control department. If there is any doubt, shut down the offending engine; you will be better off with the zero drag of a

Figure 7-1

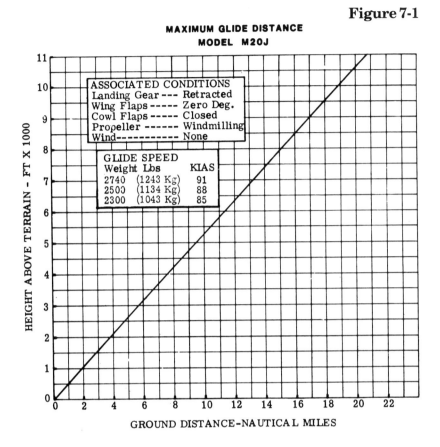

MAXIMUM GLIDE DISTANCE
MODEL M20J

ASSOCIATED CONDITIONS
Landing Gear --- Retracted
Wing Flaps ----- Zero Deg.
Cowl Flaps ----- Closed
Propeller ------ Windmilling
Wind---------- None

GLIDE SPEED

Weight Lbs		KIAS
2740	(1243 Kg)	91
2500	(1134 Kg)	88
2300	(1043 Kg)	85

HEIGHT ABOVE TERRAIN - FT X 1000

GROUND DISTANCE-NAUTICAL MILES

feathered propeller than with the questionable power output of a sick engine.

Straight Ahead, or Turn Back

Even the earliest powered-airplane pilots probably recognized the wisdom of landing straight ahead when the only engine quit close to the ground after takeoff. Of course the Wright brothers and immediate followers had little choice—their airplanes assumed the aerodynamic characteristics of grand pianos without power, and no matter what they did, impact was going to take place very shortly.

The universally accepted practice is (1) land straight ahead

Figure 7-2

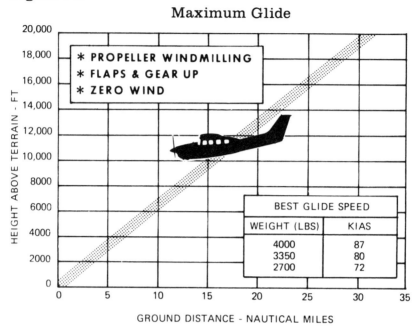

Maximum Glide

GROUND DISTANCE - NAUTICAL MILES

when the engine quits immediately after takeoff. Small changes in heading—perhaps 30 degrees or so—are permitted to reach a more favorable landing site if the failure occurs after "sufficient" altitude has been gained. You can return to the airport if you have "enough" altitude—or words to that effect. The fly in the ointment is your definition of "sufficient" and "enough." What's good for the goose is not necessarily good for the gander, as the old saying goes, because we're dealing with a wide variety of pilot personalities, proficiencies and airplane performance.

There are a couple of factors that have major inputs to the question of how much altitude is sufficient or enough. First is the timing; if you are mentally prepared for an engine failure and are willing to make the right moves *right now,* you might be able to get back to the runway, or at least the airport surface, which is almost preferable to landing off-airport. Next is bank angle and coordination; are you willing to roll the airplane up on a wing to the extent necessary to accomplish the turn? Keep in mind, of course, that the steeper the bank, the greater the bite it takes out of gliding distance and your margin above stall speed. A very steep bank that just

Figure 7-3

MAXIMUM GLIDE

CONDITIONS:
1. Landing Gear - UP.
2. Wing Flaps - UP.
3. Propellers - FEATHERED.
4. Best Glide Speed.
5. Zero Wind.

BEST GLIDE SPEED

WEIGHT POUNDS	KIAS
7450	122
6800	116
6200	111
5600	105

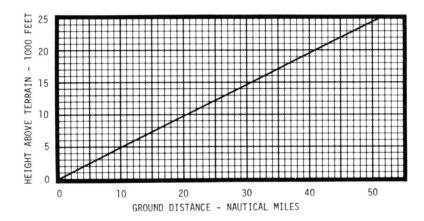

barely gets you back to the airport might be so steep that you won't have time to roll out before touchdown; not a pretty arrival.

A third factor that must be considered is the amount of turn required. A 180 simply won't do it, because a half-circle will put you beside the runway. Depending on wind conditions, you may need to turn 270 degrees, or even 360 degrees in order to line up with an acceptable landing surface.

There are so many variables in this emergency procedure that we cannot recommend any one procedure that will always work. What we can recommend is that you experiment—at a safe altitude, of course—with various airspeeds, bank angles, turn rates and timing considerations to develop altitude limits that for you will be "sufficient" and "enough." Don't be surprised to discover that 1,000 feet or more is required to get the job done safely, even in the most favorable circumstances.

Oh, yes—when in doubt, land straight ahead.

Airspeed, Airspeed, Airspeed

Soaring birds are the world's finest airspeed controllers. Sure, it's instinctive, but these creatures are able to maintain flight for extended periods of time by gaining altitude efficiently in rising air and giving up height very grudgingly when they run out of lift.

Slippin' and Slidin'

Many multi-engine pilots are under the impression that in "coordinated" flight, the airplane flies straight through the air, without slipping or skidding. That may be true in a single-engine airplane or a twin with equal power on both sides. But when one engine quits, and the power is off-center, the rules suddenly change.

In fact, in wings-level "coordinated" flight—with the ball precisely centered—an engine-out twin is flying at a rather large sideslip (below left). A piece of string taped to the nose or windshield would lean toward the good engine. Single-engine rate of climb degrades drastically or disappears altogether, while Vmc can increase as much as 15 or 20 knots.

Naturally, when the manufactures do their performance testing to write the numbers in the owner's manual, they use precise sideslip-indicating instruments to assure zero sideslip and therefore maxi-

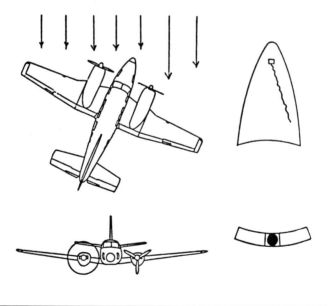

Sailplane pilots do the same thing with the help of precision flight instruments (some of the really good ones may approach the instinctive nature of the feathered folks!), but the point remains that every wing—whether built of bones or aluminum—is responsive to one airspeed that produces the most lift and the least drag simultaneously.

---

mum performance. Unfortunately, these instruments are not available to the average pilot, and he has no way of knowing his sideslip angle. (Most mistakenly assume zero sideslip occurs with wings level and the ball centered, as it does in normal flight.)

In most twins, zero sideslip occurs when the aircraft is banked approximately 5 degrees into the good engine (below right). The ball will be well off center (toward the good engine)—a fact that may disturb many pilots—but a yawstring will show that the airflow is straight along the nose, the proper flow for minimum drag and maximum performance.

We urge multi-engine pilots to tape a piece of string or yarn to the nose of their aircraft and go out and try some single-engine flight. You may be surprised. Frankly, we believe that a piece of red yarn and duct tape should be mandatory equipment on any twin-engine airplane. But we wonder if it would have to be TSOed....

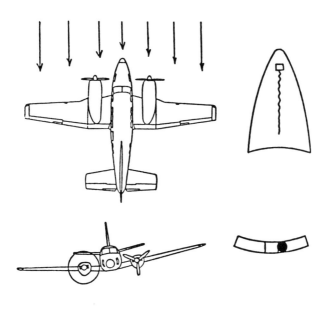

That may be a bit over-generalized for aerodynamic engineers, but most pilots need to be acutely aware of that airspeed for the airplane(s) they fly; the onset of engine problems, or a sudden unexpected failure is no time to be digging through the POH in search of the airspeed that will save your neck.

Single-engine airplane handbooks usually prescribe one speed for maximum glide, not because it's a magic number, but because the weight range of small aircraft is not very large, and weight has a significant effect on best-glide speed. Figure 7-1 is a typical single-engine Maximum Glide chart, and the 83 knots quoted will not be far off the mark for this airplane at any weight. The conscientious pilot who really wants to get the most glide distance should experiment in flight at various weights and make a table of airspeeds for his own use.

Larger airplanes with a lot of pounds between "empty weight" and "maximum takeoff weight" will have a corresponding range of airspeeds for maximum glide with various loads, as in Figures 7-2 and 7-3.

The interesting point here is that slower is not better when it comes to gliding as far as possible. As airspeed is decreased, more drag is generated and wipes out the lift-producing advantage of the higher angle of attack. The airspeed that produces maximum glide distance represents the most effective combination of lift (which must be maintained) and drag (which cannot be eliminated), resulting in the greatest number of miles covered for each increment of altitude lost. Most single-engine airplanes will glide one and a half, maybe two miles forward for each 1,000 feet of altitude (AGL, of course); we cannot emphasize strongly enough that glide performance is subject to a host of variables, and chart distances are attainable only when all the conditions (including the level of piloting skill) are optimized. That seldom is the case.

If nothing else, it's worthwhile to have an idea of how far your airplane might be expected to glide. Check the chart, add a big fudge factor for variables you can't control, and at least you'll be able to make a more intelligent decision when you select an altitude for crossing a mountain range or a large body of water.

A Word About Zero Sideslip

Just as maximum glide performance depends on good airspeed control, engine-out performance in any multi-engine airplane (except those categorized "centerline thrust") depends heavily on the pilot's ability to reduce sideslip to zero. It's a matter of effective management of resources, and some explanation is in order.

Whenever all of a twin's thrust is being developed on one side, the airplane is literally being dragged through the air with considerable sideslip (see sidebar on pages 166 and 167). This is because the asymmetric thrust is constantly trying to yaw the airplane toward the dead engine, and also because of the side force generated by the rudder as the pilot pushes the pedal to the floor to maintain straight flight. If airspeed is permitted to get so low that the fully deflected rudder can't compensate for the asymmetric thrust, the airplane will yaw and turn toward the dead engine.

To help offset these two sideways vectors and ease some of the rudder's load, the airplane can be banked a bit away from the dead engine, thereby creating a horizontal component of the wing's lift and permitting the rudder to do its work at a lower airspeed. The amount of bank is a critical value, and for most light twins it's on the order of two to five degrees. Look closely in the POH section dealing with engine-out procedures, and you'll find the value appropriate for your airplane.

The performance figures for multi-engine airplanes in an engine-out configuration are based on zero sideslip (the result of employing the slight bank to offset asymmetric thrust), and rate of climb will suffer remarkably—may well disappear entirely—unless this procedure is used.

It's not easy to do, because you must hold the airplane in the banked attitude, and not all light twins have aileron trim to give you a hand. Suffice it to say that unless your instinctive reaction to an engine failure is an immediate "lock" on heading and a concurrent bank away from the suspect engine, it's time to schedule some dual with an experienced multi-engine instructor and get your engine-out proficiency rehoned.

Index